# Fifty Movies You May Not Have Seen That You Should

Derek Zemrak

BearManor Media

Orlando, Florida

***Fifty Movies You May Have Not Seen That You Should***
© 2021 Derek Zemrak. All Rights Reserved.

No portion of this publication may be reproduced, stored, and/or copied electronically (except for academic use as a source), nor transmitted in any form or by any means without the prior written permission of the publisher and/or author.

 Published in the USA by
BearManor Media
1317 Edgewater Dr. #110
Orlando, FL 32804
www.BearManorMedia.com

Softcover Edition
ISBN: 978-1-62933-704-3

Printed in the United States of America

# Filmography

| Movie | Page | Watched |
|---|---|---|
| *My Own Private Idaho* (1991) | 1 | ☐ |
| *The Man in the Moon* (1991) | 2 | ☐ |
| *What's Eating Gilbert Grape* (1993) | 4 | ☐ |
| *Before Sunrise* (1995) | 6 | ☐ |
| *The Spitfire Grill* (1996) | 7 | ☐ |
| *Cats Don't Dance* (1997) | 9 | ☐ |
| *The Mighty* (1998) | 11 | ☐ |
| *The Opposite of Sex* (1997) | 12 | ☐ |
| *Waking Ned Devine* (1998) | 14 | ☐ |
| *You Can Count on Me* (2000) | 16 | ☐ |
| *Ghost World* (2001) | 18 | ☐ |
| *In the Bedroom* (2001) | 19 | ☐ |
| *The Majestic* (2001) | 21 | ☐ |
| *Standing in the Shadows of Motown* (2002) | 23 | ☐ |
| *Monster* (2003) | 25 | ☐ |
| *Shattered Glass* (2003) | 26 | ☐ |
| *The Station Agent* (2003) | 28 | ☐ |
| *Mean Creek* (2004) | 30 | ☐ |
| *Millions* (2004) | 32 | ☐ |
| *The Woodsman* (2004) | 34 | ☐ |
| *The Squid and the Whale* (2005) | 35 | ☐ |
| *Hollywoodland* (2006) | 37 | ☐ |
| *Death at a Funeral* (2007) | 39 | ☐ |
| *Once* (2007) | 41 | ☐ |

| | | |
|---|---:|:---:|
| *The Final Season* (2007) | 43 | ☐ |
| *Lovely, Still* (2008) | 44 | ☐ |
| *Mary and Max* (2009) | 46 | ☐ |
| *The Mighty Macs* (2009) | 48 | ☐ |
| *Flipped* (2010) | 49 | ☐ |
| *Bernie* (2011) | 51 | ☐ |
| *Carnage* (2011) | 53 | ☐ |
| *Submarine* (2010) | 54 | ☐ |
| *Win Win* (2011) | 56 | ☐ |
| *Frankenweenie* (2012) | 58 | ☐ |
| *The Sapphires* (2012) | 59 | ☐ |
| *Fading Gigolo* (2013) | 61 | ☐ |
| *Locke* (2013) | 63 | ☐ |
| *Parkland* (2013) | 64 | ☐ |
| *The Spectacular Now* (2013) | 66 | ☐ |
| *Chef* (2014) | 68 | ☐ |
| *Mr. Turner* (2014) | 70 | ☐ |
| *St. Vincent* (2014) | 71 | ☐ |
| *Me and Earl and the Dying Girl* (2015) | 73 | ☐ |
| *Tab Hunter Confidential* (2015) | 75 | ☐ |
| *Trumbo* (2015) | 76 | ☐ |
| *Sing Street* (2016) | 78 | ☐ |
| *Finding Your Feet* (2017) | 80 | ☐ |
| *Beautiful Boy* (2018) | 82 | ☐ |

| | | |
|---|---|---|
| *The Bill Murray Stories: Life Lessons Learned from a Mythical Man* (2018) | 84 | ☐ |
| *The Peanut Butter Falcon* (2019) | 85 | ☐ |

Index           91

Every book starts with an idea.

The origin of this book came from film aficionado, Marcus Siu. It was through Marcus's persistence that this book got started. Thank you.

Author, Josephine (Jo) Mele, made it complete. As a development editor, I can only imagine the numerous hours Jo spent reading, editing, and crafting suggestions. Many thanks, Jo.

A special thank you to Joseph Cabrera for taking the time to confirm and cross reference the names of the cast and crew of each film.

I would also like to thank artist Dave Woodman for designing a cover that captures the true spirit of the book.

And finally, thank you Leonard Pirkle for the final pass through of the book.

Dedicated to my mother,

Antoinette "Toni" Zemrak,

who took me to my first movie when I was five:

the 1971 rerelease of Walt Disney's *Pinocchio*.

# Foreword

I have known Derek Zemrak for many years, and he is without question one of the world's great movie lovers. As he has been a film critic for over twenty years, I can imagine the countless times people have asked him, "What are your favorite movies?"

Derek's probable response: "Movies are like wine—so many varieties and everyone's palate is different."

According to the Internet Movie Database (IMDB), on average, about 2,600 movies have been produced each year since 1900. And when you consider that modern technology (such as improved cameras, sound and editing equipment, and drones) has vastly improved the ability of more filmmakers to emerge. In recent years, over nine thousand movies have been produced annually. No one can possibly see them all.

I imagine that's what led Derek to write this book. He has gathered more than a few movies you may not have seen, or others you'd like to revisit. Perhaps you will find a hidden gem in the vast pile of films produced. His list represents outstanding films that are a treat to discover.

He has included dramas, comedy, coming of age (his favorite genre), animation, and documentaries in this collection. Some are major studio releases, and others are independent films that never made it to larger movie theaters.

Compiling this list could not have been an easy task narrowing the list down to fifty movies and, like wine, some you will like, and some you won't.

I am sure you will find several that you will enjoy—and a few that you will absolutely love.

Enjoy,
David Mickey Evans, director/writer, *The Sandlot, Radio Flyer*

**1.** *My Own Private Idaho* (1991)
Director: Gus Van Sant
Drama
104 minutes
R

*My Own Private Idaho* is the second feature film directed by Oscar winner Gus Van Sant (*Milk, Good Will Hunting*). The story follows Michael, a gay narcoleptic hustler, portrayed by the talented late actor River Phoenix (*Stand By Me*). Michael suffers from extreme loneliness, a result of his abandonment as a child. He lives on the streets with his only friend, Scott (Keanu Reeves, *The Matrix*). Scott is a bisexual hustler from a wealthy family. Michael is secretly in love with Scott, and their relationship takes a turn on their travels to Italy.

The film is a raw, painful movie that addresses homelessness, teen runaways, drug abuse, and prostitution. It contains several nude scenes (making it not for everyone), and it showcases the talent evident in the early careers of Van Sant, Phoenix, and Reeves.

Van Sant wrote the screenplay loosely based on Shakespeare's *Henry IV, Part 1*; *Henry IV, Part 2*; and *Henry V*. The script shows Van Sant's talent as one of the most prolific screenwriters of modern times. The title came to Van Sant from the B-52's song "Private Idaho," and the film showcases Van Sant's eye for quality cinematography.

Phoenix was twenty-one when the movie, perhaps his greatest role, was filmed; it was one of the last films he made before his tragic death in 1993. He earned a Best Male Lead Actor Award at the 1992 Independent Film Spirit Awards. Reeves also gives a memorable performance in a role that required a wide range of acting skill. Van Sant brought out the best of both young actors.

*My Own Private Idaho* was nominated for six Independent Film Spirit Awards in 1992 for the following: Best Male Lead (Phoenix), Best Director (Van Sant), Best Film Music (Bill Stafford), Best Cinematography (Eric Alan Edwards, John J. Campbell), Best Screenplay (Van Sant), and Best Feature (Laurie

Parker). The film won three awards for Best Lead Male, Best Screenplay, and Best Film Music.

**2. *The Man in the Moon*** (1991)
Director: Robert Mulligan
Drama
99 minutes
PG-13

*The Man in the Moon* is an important coming-of-age film centered around the main character, a fifteen-year-old girl. Often, movies concentrating on the awkward transition phase between childhood and adulthood are centered around boys. *The Man in the Moon* is one of the best to address this subject matter.

Actress Reese Witherspoon at a Hollywood premiere early in her career.
Photo Credit: Paul Smith / Featureflash.com

Dani (Reese Witherspoon, *Walk the Line*), a fifteen-year-old girl, falls in love with Court (Jason London, *Dazed and Confused*), a seventeen-year-old boy. She experiences her first kiss and seeks advice from her older sister, Maureen (Emily Warfield, *Days of Our Lives*). As time goes on, she can see that Court is more interested in Maureen than in her. How can she ever forgive her sister?

The dialogue between Dani and her mother, Oscar nominee Tess Harper (*Crimes of the Heart*), winner of a California Independent Film Festival Lifetime Achievement Award (2012), is something that all mothers and daughters should share. This movie explores not only the mother-daughter relationship but also those of siblings.

*The Man in the Moon* will make you remember your teen years, both the happy moments and the sad. Although the movie is set in the 1950s, it still holds up today, as it will for generations to come.

The movie introduced to the big screen a young actress named Reese Witherspoon. Her performance at the age of fifteen showed that she had the ability to become an Oscar-winning actress. Fifteen years later in 2006, she won an Oscar for her role as June Cash in *Walk the Line*. Reese attended an open casting call for extras for the movie but ended with one of the leading roles.

This drama was directed by Oscar nominee Robert Mulligan, who also directed the classic film *To Kill a Mockingbird*. *The Man in the Moon* was Mulligan's final film; he passed away in 2008. Mulligan superbly directs this film from the actors to the emotional roller-coaster ride that this well-balanced script provides. The movie was filmed in Louisiana, and the rural setting gives the film a sense of innocence that is significant to the picture.

The movie was produced by Oscar nominee Mark Rydell (*On Golden Pond*). Rydell was honored at the 2009 California Independent Film Festival with a Golden Slate Award.

**3. *What's Eating Gilbert Grape* (1993)**
Director: Lasse Hallstrom
Drama
118 minutes
PG-13

*What's Eating Gilbert Grape* is a story of accepting who you are and the importance of family. It was an adapted screenplay from the 1991 novel of the same name, directed by Oscar-nominated director Lasse Hallstrom (*The Cider House Rules* and *My Life as a Dog*).

Gilbert (Johnny Depp, *Chocolat*), lives in the small town of Endora, Iowa. He questions his being as he spends his days working at the local grocery store stocking shelves. Gilbert also takes care of his mentally disabled brother Arnie (Leonardo DiCaprio, *The Revenant*). He has been the head of the household since his father committed suicide seven years earlier. His mother (Darlene Cates, *Billboard*), a former beauty queen, has not been able to leave the house since her husband's death and is battling obesity. Gilbert sees no way out until a stranger (Juliette Lewis, *Cape Fear*) comes into town and brings him hope.

*What's Eating Gilbert Grape* is a film worth seeing for the quality of the story and the performances of the cast. Each cast member was believable and touching in so many ways, but it's DiCaprio who is the standout.

DiCaprio, only eighteen, gave the performance of a lifetime as Arnie pure acting excellence for not only his line delivery, but for his body movements and facial expressions. DiCaprio received several accolades for the role, including both a Best Supporting Actor nomination from the Golden Globes and an Oscar nomination. DiCaprio was robbed of the Oscar in 1995. This could be one of the biggest Oscar snubs of all time a real shame.

Actor Leonardo DiCaprio in 1994.
Photo Credit: Paul Smith / Featureflash.com

**4.** *Before Sunrise* (1995)
Director: Richard Linklater
Romantic Drama
101 minutes
R

Richard Linklater is a self-taught filmmaker and a master at making movies about real life. He has addressed the many stages of life throughout his filmmaking career with such films as *Boyhood*, *Dazed and Confused* and *Everyone Wants Some!!* Linklater is a true storyteller.

*Before Sunrise* has been mentioned numerous times as one of the most romantic films of all time. I would go even further and say that it is *the* most romantic independent film ever made.

Actress Julie Delpy and actor Ethan Hawke at a Los Angeles premiere.
Photo Credit: Paul Smith / Featureflash.com

It's a simple story of two strangers, Jesse (Ethan Hawke, *Training Day*), an American, and Céline (Julie Delpy, *Three Colors: White*), a French university student, and their chance meeting on a train. Jesse convinces Céline to spend the day with him in Vienna. As they explore, they get to know each other by asking basic life questions. Their feelings grow deeper with each honest answer received. The obstacle? Jesse is heading to America the following day.

The brilliant script will keep you engaged during the entire film. Linklater said that Delpy wrote much of the dialogue, which gives it a raw, spontaneous, and realistic feel. The chemistry between Hawke and Delpy is perfection.

Although *Before Sunrise* did not receive a major film award, it did win Linklater a Best Director Award at the 1995 Berlin International Film Festival.

*Before Sunrise* is a stunning and realistic movie that started the independent film movement.

**5. *The Spitfire Grill* (1996)**
Director: Lee David Zlotoff
Drama
117 minutes
PG-13

When Percy Talbots (Alison Elliott, *The Wings of the Dove*) is released from prison, she starts looking for a fresh start in life. She decides to move to the small rural town of Gillead, Maine. When Percy arrives, she gets a job at the local diner. The Spitfire Grill is owned by longtime resident Hannah, played by Oscar winner Ellen Burstyn (*Alice Doesn't Live Here Anymore*).

Percy befriends Shelby, a waitress portrayed by Oscar and Tony winner Marcia Gay Harden (*Pollock*). The three ladies build a sisterhood. The rest of Gillead's residents question Percy's motives.

Hannah plans to retire but worries about what will happen to the only restaurant in town. Percy gives her the idea of having a writing contest to choose the new owner of the Spitfire Grill. Contestants need to submit a letter detailing why they want to own the diner. There is a $25 submission fee. Percy had learned of this type of contest while working at a call center during her time in prison.

The ladies are amazed and highly amused by the numbers of letters and money pouring in for a chance to win the diner. A nosy postal worker (Louise De Cormier, *Ethan Frome*) wants to find out why so many letters are being delivered to Hannah. When Percy meets the local hermit living in the woods, rumors start to fly throughout the community. Trust is being questioned by many, and the small town is torn apart.

*The Spitfire Grill* won the grand prize at the Sundance Film Festival in 1996. The acting is top notch, with Ellen Burstyn playing an eighty-year-old. Burstyn in the role of Hannah with a perfect Maine accent and the body movements of a person thirty years her senior—displays genuine acting brilliance.

A little fun fact: Gillead, Maine, is a real town in Maine, spelled Gilead. The movie was shot in Peacham, Vermont. The scenery truly captures the essence of Maine through the stunning landscape, houses, and the wonderful cinematography of Rob Draper.

Actress Ellen Burstyn
Photo Credit: Paul Smith / Featureflash.com

**6. *Cats Don't Dance* (1997)**
Director: Mark Dindal
Animation
75 minutes
G

*Cats Don't Dance* is set in the 1930s, the golden age of Hollywood. Danny (voiced by Scott Bakula, *Quantum Leap*) is a handsome, stylish young cat with all the right moves who dreams of becoming a movie star. He leaves his hometown of Kokomo on a bus for Hollywood to embark on his quest. Danny has a checklist laying out his "Schedule to Stardom" that he carries to keep him on track toward his goal.

When Danny arrives in Hollywood and exits the bus, you will be entertained by his singing and dancing through the streets. Caricature cameos are seen from Hollywood legends including Bette Davis, Mae West, W. C. Fields, Jimmy Durante, Stan Laurel and Oliver Hardy. Amazing songs written by two-time Oscar winner and seven-time Grammy winner Randy Newman (*Toy Story 3*, *Monsters, Inc*) are featured in this musical animation.

When Danny makes it to Hollywood, the next thing on his checklist is finding an agent. The first agency specializes in animals. There, Danny makes several new friends, a group of aging animal actors who once had the same dream of being stars in Hollywood. As luck would have it, the agency is currently casting animals for the next Darla Dimple film. Darla (Ashley Peldon, *Drop Dead Fred*) is the princess of Tinseltown, and her movies are pure gold for Mammoth Studios. Danny lands the part of a cat in the movie. He will be in a scene with the agency's receptionist, Sawyer (Jasmine Guy, *Harlem Nights*).

Danny is shocked to learn that his only line is "Meow," but that is not going to stop him. During the shoot, Danny takes things into his own hands and expands his role to show off his singing and dancing talent. This completely upsets the ultramoody star, Darla. Along with her Lurchlike assistant, Max (voiced by the director, Mark Dindal), she vows to destroy Danny's career.

*Cats Don't Dance* is a charming, animated film that was lost during the wave of major studios moving to 3-D animated films. The animation is superb, with vibrant colors showcasing a combination of Warner Bros. and Disney animation styles. The voice talent is fun and energetic, which results in audiences loving each character. Kathy Najimy (*Sister Act*) as Tillie Hippo will have you laughing, and Betty Lou Gerson, best known as Cruella de Vil (*One Hundred and One Dalmatians*), is a real delight as Frances, a Joan Crawford-like fish.

The nostalgia of Hollywood's golden age shines in the screenplay from the caricature cameos of artist Dave Woodman, to the details of the historic Grauman's Chinese Theatre. Hollywood Legend Gene Kelly (*Singin' in the Rain*) was the consultant and choreographer for all the dance sequences in the movie, and it shows.

Do yourself a big favor and see this animated film.

**7. *The Mighty*** (1998)
Director: Peter Chelsom
Drama/Comedy
100 minutes
PG-13

Max (Elden Henson, *Daredevil*) is a teen who lives with his grandparents (Gena Rowlands, *The Notebook*) and Harry Dean Stanton, *Alien*). Due to his tragic past, he doesn't like to speak or socialize. He has no friends and is unable to read.

Things began to change for Max when a disabled thirteen-year-old boy named Kevin (Kieran Culkin, *Succession*) and his mom (Sharon Stone, *Casino*) move next door. Kevin becomes Max's reading tutor, and they both learn from the book *King Arthur and His Knights of the Round Table*. Kevin suggest that they combine each other's strengths to overcome their weaknesses.

Actress Sharon Stone
Photo Credit: Paul Smith / Featureflash.com

As the two young boys embark on their courageous adventures, they learn the power of kindness. Kevin encourages Max to live by the words in King Arthur's book: a knight proves his worthiness through his deeds. Through their adventures they discover the greatest treasure of all: friendship.

*The Mighty* is a heartwarming story about acceptance and kindness. The boys learn that everyone has strengths and weaknesses and that they should give people a chance.

Additional supporting cast includes Gillian Anderson (*The X-Files*), James Gandolfini (*The Sopranos*), and musician Meatloaf. *The Mighty* is an uplifting film that will pull on your heartstrings.

*The Mighty* received two Golden Globe nominations in 1999: Best Supporting Actress for Sharon Stone and Best Original Song, "The Mighty," by Sting and Trevor Jones.


**8. *The Opposite of Sex* (1997)**
Director: Don Roos
Comedy/Drama
105 minutes
R

*The Opposite of Sex* is a dark comedy about a rebellious sixteen-year-old girl.

Dedee is portrayed by Christina Ricci (*Monster*, *The Addams Family*). After the death of her stepfather, Dedee decides to move in with her wealthy gay half-brother, Bill (Martin Donovan, *Big Little Lies*, *Weeds*). Bill is still mourning the death of his longtime partner, who died of AIDS.

Dedee has plans of her own. She seduces Bill's current boyfriend, Matt (Ivan Sergei, *Jack & Jill*), and informs him that she is pregnant. After telling Bill and Tom's high-strung sister Lucia (Lisa Kudrow, *Friends*), who is secretly in love with Bill, of the pregnancy, Dedee and Matt steal ten thousand dollars from Bill and run off to Los Angeles.

When Matt's ex-lover, Jason (Johnny Galecki, *The Big Bang Theory*), learns of Matt's disappearance, he accuses Bill, his former teacher, of molestation to blackmail him into locating Matt and Dedee. With his reputation on the line, Bill tracks down the missing couple with the help of Lucia and the local sheriff, played by three-time Grammy Award winner and Golden Globe Award recipient Lyle Lovett.

Actress Christina Ricci at the 1999 Golden Globe Awards in Beverly Hills.
Photo Credit: Paul Smith / Featureflash.com

*The Opposite of Sex* was written and directed by Don Roos (*Boys on the Side, Marley & Me*). He does an excellent job transporting his well-written script to the big screen. There are a lot of moving parts and characters in his complicated screenplay.

Christina Ricci received a Golden Globe nomination in 1999 for her terrific performance as Dedee, a tremendously complex role with multiple layers.

*The Opposite of Sex* was nominated for four Film Independent Spirit Awards in 1999: Best First Feature (Don Roos, David Paul Kirkpatrick, Michael Besman), Best Screenplay (Don Roos), Best Female Lead (Christina Ricci), and Best Supporting Female (Lisa Kudrow). It won Best First Feature and Best Screenplay.

**9. *Waking Ned Devine* (1998)**
Director: Kirk Jones
Comedy
91 minutes
PG

Someone in a small, quaint village in Ireland with a population of fifty-two residents has just won the lottery. But who is it?

Jackie (Ian Bannen, *The Flight of the Phoenix*), a fast-talking resident, is determined to find out who the winner is with the help from his buddy Michael (David Kelly, *Charlie and the Chocolate Factory*).

They embark on eliminating residents one at a time. After disqualifying a few, Jackie and Michael decide to pay Ned Devine a visit. When they get to his rural home, they discover him dead in his living room chair. He is holding the winning lottery ticket and has a smile on his face. It seems that poor Ned died of a heart attack from the excitement of winning the lottery.

Jackie quickly convinces Michael to call the lottery headquarters and say that he is Ned Devine and is ready to turn over the winning ticket for the jackpot. Will the two best friends be able to pull it off?

They have a few obstacles: Ned signed the back of the winning ticket, and they have to deal with Jackie's wife Annie, (Fionnula Flanagan, *Rich Man, Poor Man*); the village bitch, Lizzy (Eileen Dromey, *Space Truckers*); and the rest of the locals.

*Waking Ned Devine* is a dark, quirky comedy that was originally set to be a ten-minute short film. Director and writer Kirk Jones decided to make the movie into a feature, and many of the cast and crew reduced their compensation to be able to keep the budget to three million dollars.

This delightfully entertaining film received two Screen Actor Award nominations in 1999 for Outstanding Performance by a Cast, and Best Actor for David Kelly.

Treat yourself and see *Waking Ned Devine* before rigor mortis sets in.

**10. *You Can Count on Me* (2000)**
Director: Kenneth Lonergan
Drama
111 minutes
R

Three-time Oscar nominee Laura Linney (*The Savages, Kinsey*) portrays Sammy, a single mom trying to keep everything together for her son. They live in the rural Catskill mountain town where she grew up.

Things get even more difficult when the bank Sammy has been working at for eight years hires Brian (Matthew Broderick, *Ferris Bueller's Day Off*), a hard-nosed boss. When Sammy is no longer allowed to leave work at 3:15 p.m. to pick up her son, Rudy (Rory Culkin, *Mean Creek*), from school, she has nowhere to turn.

After months of not hearing from her wayward brother, Terry (Mark Ruffalo, *Spotlight*), he shows up in town and agrees to take on the responsibility of caring for Rudy. The two build a special bond even though Terry sometimes pushes the limits and forces Sammy to make difficult decisions.

Ever since Sammy and Terry lost their parents in a car accident at young age, they had a pact to always be there for each other. Will the siblings be able to hold up their end of the deal?

*You Can Count on Me* received positive reviews from critics and at film festivals but only grossed $11 million at movie theaters in 2000. The acting is top notch. Laura Linney received a Golden Globe and an Oscar nomination for her role as Sammy.

The film won the Grand Prize Jury Award for Dramatic Feature and Best Screenplay (Kenneth Lonergan) at the 2000 Sundance Film Festival.

*You Can Count on Me* swept the 2001 Film Independent Spirit Awards, winning the two major categories, Best First Feature, and Best Screenplay (Lonergan). Linney received a Best Female Lead nomination. Ruffalo was nominated for Best Male Lead. Rory Culkin was nominated for Best Debut Performance, which was much deserved.

*You Can Count on Me* is a film about a family and their daily struggles, a true independent film shot on a budget of $1.2 million. This film was loved by critics but wasn't well received at the box office. It is worth a watch, and I know you will not be disappointed.

You'll wonder how this movie was not a big box-office success.

Actress Laura Linney at the 2001 Golden Globe Awards at the Beverly Hilton Hotel.
Photo Credit: Paul Smith / Featureflash.com

**11.** *Ghost World* (2001)
Director: Terry Zwigoff
Comedy/Drama
111 minutes
R

This is the only movie in this book that originated from a comic book. *Ghost World* is based on a graphic novel by Daniel Clowes of the same title.

The movie takes place after the high school graduation of two best friends, Enid (Thora Birch, *Hocus Pocus*) and Rebecca (Scarlett Johansson, *Marriage Story*), who are planning their future. They are ready to take on the world and have no plan to attend college. The idea of being roommates is derailed when Enid must attend a summer class to receive her diploma. Rebecca takes a job at a coffee shop to begin her working career.

The girls decide to play a mean trick on a guy who wrote a missed-connection ad in the local paper. Their lives are changed forever. The man who placed the ad is Seymour (Steve Buscemi, *Fargo*), a geeky vinyl record collector looking for love. The girls soon discover the complexities of the real world. Although Enid and Rebecca have been besties their entire lives, their perspectives on life are soon headed down different paths.

The ensemble is pure casting magic with Birch, Johansson, and Buscemi. Their performances are real, natural, and believable. Birch and Buscemi received Best Supporting Actor nominations at the 2002 Golden Globes.

Buscemi won the 2002 Film Independent Spirit Award for Best Supporting Actor, and the film won Best First Screenplay for Clowes and Zwigoff. The film also received a Best First Feature nomination for Terry Zwigoff.

This independent film went on to receive an Oscar nomination for Best Adapted Screenplay in 2002. Clowes and Zwigoff also received an Oscar nomination in 2002 for Best Writing. Screenplay Based on Material Previously Produced or Published.

You'll want to see this film more than once to appreciate how masterfully the end of the movie was crafted throughout the entire film. *Ghost World* is a diamond to be discovered in Hollywood's pile of cubic zirconia.

Fifty Movies You May Not Have Seen That You Should

**12.** *In the Bedroom* (2001)
Director: Todd Field
Crime/Drama
131 minutes
R

*In the Bedroom* revolves around the family drama of doctor Matt Fowler (Tom Wilkinson, *Michael Clayton*); his wife, Ruth (Sissy Spacek, *Coal Miner's Daughter*); and their son, Frank (Nick Stahl, *The Man Without a Face*), who are all going through transitions in their lives.

Frank is preparing to leave Maine to attend college, but all is derailed when he has a passionate love affair with an older single mom, Natalie (Marisa Tomei, *My Cousin Vinny*).

Their quiet town in Maine is turned upside down when Natalie's ex-husband, Richard (William Mapother, *Lost*) can't deal with his ex being involved with a younger man. As the Maine weather begins to make the transition from the beautiful summer to the darker fall and winter ahead, the movie transforms flawlessly into a dark thriller.

Few directors can hit a home run on their debut film, but Todd Field accomplished a walk-off homer in the bottom of the ninth with *In the Bedroom*. The film was marvelously assembled, from its astonishing cast to the inventive direction of a master storyteller.

Actress Sissy Spacek at the 59th Annual Golden Globe Awards in Beverly Hills.
Photo Credit: Paul Smith / Featureflash.com

As one of the best indie films ever produced in American cinema history, *In the Bedroom* was not overlooked by the Academy of Arts and Sciences. It earned five Oscar nominations in 2002, including Best Picture (Graham Leader, Ross Katz, Todd Field), Best Adapted Screenplay (Todd Field, Robert Festinger), Best Actress (Spacek), Best Actor (Wilkinson), and Best Supporting Actress (Tomei). Sadly, *In the Bedroom* did not win any Oscars.

Sissy Spacek won her third Best Actress Golden Globe for her role of Ruth, and Marisa Tomei received a Best Supporting Actress Golden Globe nomination for her standout portrayal of Natalie.

The film walked away with three Film Independent Spirit Awards winning, Best First Feature (Todd Field), Best Actress (Sissy Spacek), and Best Actor (Tom Wilkinson). It also earned a nomination for Best Screenplay (Robert Festinger, Todd Field).

**13.** *The Majestic* (2001)
Director: Frank Darabont
Drama/Romance
152 minutes
PG

Peter Appleton (Jim Carrey, *The Mask*) is a blacklisted Hollywood screenwriter who has amnesia as a result of an automobile accident. Peter finds himself in a small town where he is mistaken for Luke Trimble, a local who was presumed killed in World War II. Together with Luke's father, Harry, played by Oscar-winning actor Martin Landau (*Ed Wood*), and the community's support, they reopen the Majestic Theatre.

Only one thing could derail Jim Carrey, one of the biggest box-office draws in 2001. That would be 9/11. *The Majestic* was to be released the week of the infamous attacks by the terrorist group al-Qaeda against the United States on the morning of Tuesday, September 11, 2001. The release was rescheduled for December 21 and was lost in the high wave of holiday movies. The film pays homage to Frank Capra films such as *It Happened One Night* and *It's a Wonderful Life*.

Carrey's performance is not the typical over-the-top zaniness you expect from him; it's an outstanding dramatic role. He should have received more recognition for what could have been the greatest role in his long film career.

Martin Landau, a master of the acting craft, never disappointed in any role he accepted. Landau's role of Harry is a special treat to witness. The ensemble cast also includes Laurie Holden (*The Walking Dead*); Oscar nominee Hal Holbrook (*Into the Wild*); two-time Oscar nominee, the brilliant; James Whitmore (*Give 'em Hell, Harry!*); and Jeffrey DeMunn (*The Green Mile*).

*The Majestic* was directed by three-time Oscar nominee Frank Darabont (*The Shawshank Redemption*, *The Green Mile*, and worldwide television series phenomenon, *The Walking Dead*).

*The Majestic* is truly one of the lost treasures in the cinematic realm.

**14.** *Standing in the Shadows of Motown* (2002)
Director: Paul Justman
Documentary/Music
108 minutes
PG

Here is a trivia question for you: What musical band had more hits than the Beatles, Elvis, the Rolling Stones, and the Beach Boys combined?

The answer? The Funk Brothers, a Detroit-based band that was chosen by Berry Gordy in 1959 as backup to the greatest Motown groups of 1959 to 1973, including the Supremes, the Temptations, the Four Tops, Gladys Knight & the Pips, Marvin Gaye, Stevie Wonder, and many more.

This unique documentary introduces the viewer to this relatively unknown band and their sound. By interweaving vintage footage, archived photos, interviews with surviving members, and tribute reenactments of their act, you get to know the Funk Brothers. They were the greatest hit machine in music history but were almost anonymous. The reenactment scenes, narrated by Andre Braugher, add to the nostalgia.

The surviving members reminisce about growing up in Detroit, meeting Berry Gordy, attending studio sessions, and touring the world nonstop. These memories make *Standing in the Shadows of Motown* a deeply personal and entertaining documentary.

The goal of this documentary was to finally bring the members of the Funk Brothers into the spotlight. It is appropriate to pay tribute to this amazingly talented group of musicians by listing their names: Richard "Pistol" Allen (drums), Jack Ashford (percussion), Bob Babbitt (bass), Benny "Papa Zita" Benjamin (drums), Eddie "Bongo" Brown (percussion), Earl Van Dyke (keyboard), Johnny Griffith (keyboard), Joe Hunter (keyboard), Uriel Jones (drums), James Jameson (bass), Robert White (guitar), and Eddie Willis (guitar). Together they were known as Detroit's hit machine.

As great as the Funk Brothers were, their run came to an end in 1973, when

Gordy made the decision to move his music empire to Los Angeles. How the band learned of the abrupt move to California will surprise you.

You'll be up on your feet dancing to the live performances from Bootsy Collins, Ben Harper, Montell Jordan, the great Chaka Khan, and others. You will be belting out Motown greatest hit songs backed up by the surviving Funk Brothers.

Sing along with the incredible songs that this amazing group of men helped create.

**15.** *Monster* (2003)
Director: Patty Jenkins
Drama/Crime
109 minutes
R

*Monster*, directed by Patty Jenkins (*Wonder Woman*), is based on the true story of Aileen Wuornos, a Florida serial killer who murdered seven men in 1989 and 1990.

Aileen (Charlize Theron, *North Country*) was a prostitute living and working the streets of Daytona, Florida. She grew up in an abusive household and was raped at the age of thirteen. When she told her dad, he didn't believe her and beat her. Her hatred toward men grew over time.

She meets a troubled young woman, Selby (Christina Ricci, *The Opposite of Sex*) at a gay bar, and they soon develop a romantic relationship. Aileen decides to quit prostitution and move out of town with Selby. When the two are unable to make ends meet, Aileen returns to the only way she knows how to make money. Her hatred for men escalates.

*Monster* is a raw, gritty film with outstanding performances from both Charlize and Christina. Charlize swept all the major awards in 2004, including an Oscar, a Golden Globe, a SAG Award, and a Film Independent Spirit Award. The accolades for one of the best physical-transformation roles in movie history are well deserved.

*Monster* was nominated for three Film Independent Spirit Awards in 2004 for Best Actress (Charlize Theron), Best First Screenplay (Patty Jenkins), and Best Feature. Charlize won Best Actress, and the film took home the Best Picture honors. At the time Charlize was an unknown actress and runway model. She transformed her runway model beauty into the monster Aileen.

After the Best Actress clip at the 2004 ceremony, people were shocked to see the gorgeous Charlize in the audience, including myself. It rates as one of the most memorable moments for me in Oscar history. *Monster* was not a blockbuster movie, but a true independent film that was produced by Charlize.

Charlize Theron at the 76th Annual Academy Awards in Hollywood.
February 29, 2004
Photo Credit: Paul Smith / Featureflash.com

**16.** *Shattered Glass* **(2003)**
Director: Billy Ray
Drama
94 minutes
PG-13

"Shattered Glass" is based on the true story of the greatest scandal in journalistic history.

Stephen Glass (Hayden Christensen, *Life as a House*) is a recent college graduate who is making a name for himself as a writer in the magazine world. In his new career, he has already written for the A-list of magazines including *Forbes, George, Harper's Magazine,* and *Rolling Stone.*

Glass is known for his colorful and humorous articles. He soon lands a job at *The New Republic,* founded in 1914, which focuses on political issues in Washington, DC. *The New Republic* is known as the in-flight magazine for Air Force One. Glass knows that the most powerful individuals in the country are reading his work.

Actor Hayden Christensen at the Los Angeles premiere *Shattered Glass.*
October 19, 2003
Photo Credit: Paul Smith / Featureflash.com

He starts pitching story lines that has everyone at the magazine impressed. It appears Glass has a golden pen. Competitive magazines began to question Glass's details in his articles. When the magazine makes an editorial change by hiring Chuck Lane (Peter Sarsgaard, *Garden State*), more questionable facts come to light.

The magazine publishes a story by Glass titled "Hack Heaven" about a teenage hacker who is hired by a software company. They decided it was better to hire him than having him continue to hack their company computers. The articles states that the teen had an agent to negotiate his deal, just like a number-one football draft pick. When the article hit the newsstands, Adam Penenberg (Steve Zahn, *War for the Planet of the Apes*), a reporter at *Forbes* digital, starts to research the story, and nothing seems to line up.

"Shattered Glass" was written and directed by Oscar nominee Billy Ray (*Captain Phillips*). The film was not a box-office success, only grossing $2.9 million worldwide, but received critical acclaim. Sarsgaard received a Best Supporting Golden Globe nomination in 2004. The film received four 2004 Film Independent Spirit Awards, including Best Feature (Craig Baumgarten, Tove Christensen, Gaye Hirsch, Adam Merims), Best Screenplay (Billy Ray), Best Cinematography (Mandy Walker), and Best Supporting Actor for Peter Sarsgaard. Although *Shattered Glass* did not win any of the awards, it is worth a watch and holds up in any political climate.

## 17. *The Station Agent* (2003)
Director: Tom McCarthy
Drama/Comedy
89 minutes
R

In 2003, a young actor with dwarfism auditioned for a part in independent film that didn't call for a dwarf. That actor was Peter Dinklage. He was so good in the audition that the production team switched the lead character in the movie to be a little person. This rewrite not only redefined the movie, but it also changed Peter's life. He later starred in HBO's acclaimed series *Game of Thrones*.

*The Station Agent* is about Finbar McBride (Dinklage), who only has one friend in the world, Henry (Paul Benjamin, *Escape from Alcatraz*), his boss at a model-train shop. After Henry's sudden death, Fin learns that his friend willed him a piece of property. It turns out to be an abandoned train depot in rural New Jersey.

Fin, a reclusive and shy person, moves into the depot where he can be alone. He plans to live a life of solitude, to no longer feel ostracized. His quiet dream life is interrupted as soon as he arrives. He meets Joe (Bobby Cannavale, *Win Win*), who is operating his father's hot dog food truck on the property.

Joe is looking for a friend to talk to about his ailing father. Olivia (Patricia Clarkson, *Pieces of April*) is a daily customer at Joe's truck. She had moved to town after the death of her two-year-old son. All three characters learn from each other and come to redefine the word *friend*.

The ensemble cast is stellar, including a small role for future four-time Oscar nominee, Michelle Williams (*Brokeback Mountain, Blue Valentine, My Week with Marilyn, Manchester by the Sea*), and a very young Raven Goodwin (*Lovely & Amazing*).

*The Station Agent* is about hardship, loneliness, and the power of friendship. It was nominated for four Film Independent Spirit Awards in 2004: for Best First Screenplay (Tom McCarthy), the John Cassavetes Award for Best Feature Produced under $500,000, a Producers Award (Mary Jane Skalski), and Best Male Lead (Peter Dinklage). It won three: Best First Screenplay, the John Cassavetes Award, and the Producers Award.

Although *The Station Agent* only grossed $8.7 million at the box office, it is one film that you should see.


**18. *Mean Creek* (2004)**
Director: Jacob Aaron Estes
Drama/Crime
90 minutes
R

*Mean Creek* is a very raw coming-of-age film. The best way to describe this movie would be *Stand By Me* meets *Deliverance*—but even grittier. Let this be your warning: *Mean Creek* is not for everyone.

Fourteen-year-old Sam (Rory Culkin, *You Can Count of Me*) informs his older brother Rocky (Trevor Morgan, *The Sixth Sense*) that he was beaten up by the school bully, George (Josh Peck, *Drake & Josh*). Rory decides to avenge his brother with the help of his friends Clyde (Ryan Kelley, *Teen Wolf*) and Marty (Scott Mechlowicz, *EuroTrip*).

They plan a fake birthday river party for Sam and invite George. Little does George know the boys are orchestrating the ultimate revenge. Sam's girlfriend, Millie (Carly Schroeder, *Gracie*), is also invited on the boating trip. When she discovers the plot against George, she asks Sam to stop the vindictive plan of retribution against George. Will the older boys agree?

The ensemble cast of young actors give raw performances that deliver mixed emotions throughout the film. Josh Peck's performance as a troubled teen with psychological issues proves his acting ability far surpasses his past roles in the

Nickelodeon kids' show *Drake and Josh*. Ryan Kelley not only commands the screen, but his performance also makes you care for this young adult who has been scarred the majority of his life.

*Mean Creek* is a dark film that proves one wrong turn in life can completely alter one's future. The cinematography establishes suspense and emptiness. The shots of weeds in the river and milky water capture the emotional loneliness of the teens.

*Mean Creek* was nominated for the C.I.C.A.E. award and the Golden Camera award at the 2004 Cannes Film Festival. In 2005, at the Film Independent Spirit Awards, it won two awards: the John Cassavetes Award and the Special Distinction Award.

If you are looking for a movie that will resonate with you for days on end, *Mean Creek* is that film. But remember I warned you.

**19.** *Millions* (2004)
Director: Danny Boyle
Comedy/Drama
98 minutes
PG

*Millions* is a movie based on Frank Cottrell Boyce's children's book of the same title. He also wrote the screenplay. It was directed by Oscar winner Danny Boyle (*Slumdog Millionaire*).

Ronnie (James Nesbitt, *Jekyll*) is looking for a fresh start after the death of his wife. He decides to move his two sons, Damian (Alex Etel, *The Water Horse*), age seven, and Anthony (Lewis McGibbon, *The Royal*), age nine, to a suburb in northern England. Moving is an adjustment for the young lads.

Damian is deeply religious and is obsessed with Catholic saints. He has all the facts about the lives of saints. He knows the miracles they performed and the torturous ways in which they died. He willingly shares this information with anyone who will listen. Many seven-year-olds can quote sports stats; Damian has saints' facts. How has Damian become an expert on saints? Well, Saint Francis, Saint Peter, and Saint Nicholas routinely appear to him for brief conversations *Millions* is not a religious movie, but religion is an important element of Damian's character.

One day when the boys are outdoors, they are shocked when a duffel bag full of British pounds falls from the sky and lands at Damian's feet. The brothers have very different visions of what they should do with the money. Damian thinks because it fell from the sky, it must be a sign from God to give it to the poor. Anthony believes they have a terrific investment opportunity in their grasp.

They have one huge problem: the British pound is due to be replaced with the euro in a few days. This act will make their bag of money worthless.

Anthony convinces his younger brother not to a say word to their dad about the loot. But their dad begins to question Damian's increased generosity and Anthony's enhanced spending. When a stranger comes looking for the money, the boys must join forces.

# Fifty Movies You May Not Have Seen That You Should

*Millions* was nominated for two British Independent Film Awards in 2005: for Best Screenplay, which it won, and Most Promising Newcomer for Alex Etel. Alex was spectacular in the role of Damian, and I am surprised his acting career never took off.

*Millions* focus is on how money can change people. The boys learn the lesson that money can generate more challenges than it is worth. This film is entertaining for children and the young at heart. Just remember, there are no pennies from heaven.

**20.** *The Woodsman* (2004)
Director: Nicole Kassell
Drama
87 minutes
R

*The Woodsman* is based on a stage play of the same name written by Steven Fechter and is the first feature film directed by Nicole Kassell (*Watchmen*).

A film about a child molester is never easy, but Kassell was able to deliver an emotional and impactful movie. Walter (Kevin Bacon, *Footloose*) is released from prison after serving twelve years for child molestation. He returns home to start a new life in Philadelphia. Walter is shunned by his family and friends except for his brother-in-law Carlos (Benjamin Bratt, *Law & Order*).

Walter rents a small apartment across the street from an elementary school, and his temptations are increasing daily. Walter gets hired at a lumber mill, where he meets coworker, Vicki (Kyra Sedgwick, *The Closer*). As their relationship grows, Walter tells Vicki about his dark past.

*The Woodsman* premiered at the Sundance Film Festival in 2004 and was nominated for a Grand Jury Award. Bacon is at the top of his acting game and is truly astonishing as Walter. He delivers a performance that is creepy, disturbing, and complex. I can only assume Bacon did not receive accolades for the role due to the subject matter.

Sedgwick, Bacon's real-life wife, was compelling as Vicki, a woman torn and caught in a web of emotions. Hannah Pilkes's portrayal of Robin, a young girl attending the elementary school, gives a staggering, impressive, and memorable performance.

The film received three Film Independent Spirit Award nominations in 2015, including Best First Feature (Nicole Kassell, Lee Daniels), Best Actor (Kevin Bacon), and Best Debut Performance (Hannah Pilkes).

*The Woodsman* is a movie you must prepare yourself to watch. It is not for everyone but worth a view for Bacon's performance. His performance is one that you will not forget.

**21. *The Squid and the Whale* (2005)**
Director: Noah Baumbach
Drama/Comedy
81 minutes
R

Divorce is never easy, especially when there are kids in the mix. *The Squid and the Whale* is loosely based on the personal experience of the director, Noah Baumbach (*Marriage Story*, *Fantastic Mr. Fox*), when his parents divorced in the early 1980s. The story focuses on the emotional impact on two teen brothers, Frank (Owen Kline, *Jobe'z World*) and Walt (Jesse Eisenberg, *The Social Network*), during their middle-class Manhattan parents' separation. Their parents, Joan (Laura Linney, *You Can Count on Me*) and Bernard (Jeff Daniels, *Something Wild*), agree to joint custody, but Frank wants to live with his mom, and Walt is for Team Dad.

The movie is painful, funny, and unforgiving. Baumbach wanted the movie to be real, so he had Daniels wear his father's old clothing. It was shot on Super 16mm film to give it more of a grainy, realistic feel.

Daniels's and Linney's performances as the egotistical father and the self-centered mom are astonishing, and earned both Golden Globe nominations. Why they didn't receive an Oscar nomination is beyond belief.

Jesse Eisenberg truly showed off his acting ability in this film. His role of Walt is raw, believable, and pure. It is worth watching the movie to witness firsthand his pure talent. Five years later in 2010, Eisenberg would be nominated for an Oscar for his role in *The Social Network*.

*The Squid and the Whale* was produced by seven-time Oscar nominee Wes Anderson (*The Royal Tenenbaums, Fantastic Mr. Fox, Moonrise Kingdom, The Grand Budapest Hotel, Isle of Dogs*). It was nominated for an Oscar in 2006 for Best Writing and for Original Screenplay for Noah Baumbach.

This film received three Golden Globe Nominations for Best Motion Picture—Comedy or Musical; Best Actor (Daniels) and Best Actress (Linney); and six nominations at the 2006 Film Independent Spirit Awards, which included Best Feature (Wes Anderson, Peter Newman, Charlie Corwin, Clara Markowicz), Best Director (Baumbach), Best Screenplay (Baumbach), Best Actor (Daniels), Best Actress (Linney), and Best Supporting Actor (Eisenberg).


**22. *Hollywoodland* (2006)**
Director: Allen Coulter
Mystery/Crime
126 minutes
R

Actor George Reeves's death on June 16, 1959, at the age of forty-five from a gunshot to the head remains one of Hollywood's most notorious unsolved mysteries. His death was ruled a suicide.

*Hollywoodland* is a fictionalization of possible circumstances surrounding the death of George Reeves. This neo-noir film centers around a fictional private detective, Louis Simo (Adrien Brody, *The Pianst*), hired by Reeves's mother (Lois Smith, *Lady Bird*) to investigate the death of her son. Simo quickly discovers that there are several things about the case the Los Angeles Police Department does not want to address.

At the time of Reeves's death, he was best known for his role of Superman in the television show *Adventures of Superman*. The show had been recently canceled, which pleased Reeves because he wanted to pursue more serious roles and wanted to direct movies.

Reeves's personal life was anything but super. He had broken off his affair with Toni Mannix (Diane Lane, *Unfaithful*), the wife of MGM studio executive Eddie Mannix (Bob Hoskins, *Mona Lisa*), for a younger aspiring actress, Leonore Lemmon (Robin Tunney, *The Craft*).

As with any classic noir film, Reeves's life had all the elements a Hollywood

crime, cynical attitudes, and sexual motivations. Was his death a suicide, or did someone want him dead?

The casting in *Hollywoodland* is spot on and earned two-time Oscar winner Ben Affleck (*Good Will Hunting*, *Argo*) a Golden Globe nomination for Best Supporting Actor in 2007. To me, I think Oscar nominee Bob Hoskins (*Mona Lisa*) was a standout in the movie for his role of Eddie Mannix. Every time he was on the screen, he controlled the scene and drew the audience in. This was not an easy task surrounded by an all-star cast. I believe this is Hoskins's finest role in a long and impressive career.

Actor Ben Affleck at the Los Angeles premiere of *Hollywoodland*.
September 7, 2006
Photo Credit: Paul Smith / Featureflash.com

If you are looking for a crime story that will a have you asking, "Whodunit?" and one that exposes the sleazy world of moviemaking, then *Hollywoodland* is the one for you.

**23. *Death at a Funeral* (2007)**
Director: Frank Oz
Comedy
90 minutes
R

First, let us clear up any confusion: this is the original British version of *Death at a Funeral*, not the 2010 Chris Rock American remake that falls subpar to the original.

Daniel (Matthew Macfadyen, *Pride & Prejudice*) is a young married man who is still living at his parents' home with his wife, Jane (Keeley Hawes, *Ashes to Ashes*), when his father unexpectedly dies. Daniel organizes his dad's funeral. Things go badly from the start, when the funeral home delivers the wrong body to the house.

What else can go wrong? Well, when you gather a completely dysfunctional family and an eclectic group of friends to attend a home funeral, you can imagine the chaos that follows.

Daniel must deal with his brother, a perceived successful author from New York who spends his last dime flying first class back to London instead of paying any of the funeral expenses. There has always been sibling rivalry between the two. It really irks Daniel when everyone at the service expects his brother to be doing the eulogy instead of him.

Daniel's grumpy old handicapped uncle is there, a cousin's fiancé mistakenly takes hallucinatory drugs, one attendee is looking to score with a woman, and then there is the mysterious little person (Pete Dinklage, *The Station Agent*), whom nobody knows. He asks to speak to Daniel privately and for him to keep everything under control.

*Death at a Funeral* is an extremely entertaining film with stellar performances from the outstanding ensemble cast. What really makes this film work is that not one actor is trying to outshine any other cast member. They have trust in the superb script written by Dean Craig, and they deliver their lines flawlessly. The comedic timing is spot on.

*Death at a Funeral* is a hilarious dark comedy directed by Frank Oz (*What About Bob?*, *The Muppets Take Manhattan*). An interesting piece of trivia: Frank Oz is the voice of Yoda in the *Star Wars* franchise films and the voice of Miss Piggy in *The Muppets*.

This is a film, much like *Waking Ned Divine*, that has you laughing out loud throughout.

**24. Once** (2007)
Director: John Carney
Romance
96 minutes
R

*Once* is a true independent film from Ireland that was shot in three weeks on a budget of $150,000. The entire production was funded by the Irish Film Board. Do not let the minuscule budget scare you away from this gem of film that is true to life and a charming romantic movie.

Glen Hansard, best known from the Irish band *The Frames*, has the lead. He plays a Dublin street musician who performs popular songs for crowds during the day and switches to his original songs in the evenings when the crowds dwindle down. One evening a young female immigrant (Marketa Irglová, *The Last Man on Earth*) from Czechoslovakia stops to listen.

Soon she is asking questions: "Who did you write that song for? Where is she? Is she alive?" At first "the guy" (we never know his name, or hers for that matter; I am assuming it was not in the budget) is perturbed with all the personal questions but quickly takes interest. As her questions continue, she discovers that his day job is repairing vacuum cleaners. As fate has it, she has a vacuum that needs repair.

The next day she returns to the same location where he is performing. She has her vacuum in tow like a dog on a leash. It is a funny, quirky scene that adds to her character. He is surprised that she showed up, but he's even more taken aback by the Hoover she brought with her and by her demands to have it repaired. After the vacuum cleaner issue is resolved, she reveals to him that she, too, is a musician. She is a classically trained pianist and writes music. Their exciting week in Dublin together includes writing, rehearsing, and recording songs about themselves.

What makes the film work is the chemistry between Hansard and Irglová. They are natural and believable on screen, and they composed all the music for the movie. Their accomplishments were not overlooked. In 2008, they won an

Academy Award for Best Achievement in Music Written for Motion Pictures for their original song "Falling Slowly."

Glen Hansard & Marketa Irglová at the 80th Annual Academy Awards at the Kodak Theatre, Hollywood, CA. February 24, 2008
Photo Credit: Paul Smith / Featureflash.com

*Once* was the winner of the Audience Award at the 2007 Sundance Film Festival and was nominated for the grand Jury Prize World Cinema Dramatic the same year. It also won the Best Foreign Film at the 2008 Film Independent Spirit Awards.

*Once* is a rare gem in cinematic history that you will find heartfelt, charismatic, and pleasant. It is a film that you will be glad you found it hits all the right notes.

**25.** *The Final Season* (2007)
Director: David Mickey Evans
Drama
119 minutes
PG

*The Final Season* is based on a true story about a high school baseball team from the small town of Norway, Iowa. The baseball powerhouse of Norway High School won nineteen state championships in twenty-two years all this talent from a town with a population of 586.

The people of Norway love their baseball team but are now faced with a problem: the school district plans to merge Norway with Madison, a much larger high school. This decision will end the team's dynasty and the town's traditions.

After the retirement of legendary head coach Jim Van Scoyoc (Powers Boothe, *Tombstone*), his assistant coach, Kent Stock (Sean Astin, *Rudy*), assumes the position. His goal is to guide the team to their twentieth Iowa State Championship.

Coach Stock has many hurdles to overcome before winning another championship in Norway's final season. Experiencing the loss of several key players due to graduation and having to earn the respect of the current players and the town are just a few of the situations confronting the new coach.

He understands the importance of baseball to the residents, and that this is what drives his team. Stock states, "We win by playing Norway baseball."

Director David Mickey Evans (*The Sandlot*) knows how to bring the love of baseball to the screen. He shows how baseball affects the small town of Norway. Community spirit is what makes *The Final Season* special.

As Coach Van Scoyoc states, "Baseball is the only game where the object is to get home." Home is where the heart is. Evans shows how hard work and respect are what built the Norway traditions for generations.

*The Final Season* is not about winning a trophy; it's about commitment, loyalty, respect, and family. This is a movie that will entertain and inspire viewers of all ages.


**26. *Lovely, Still* (2008)**
Director: Nicholas Fackler
Drama/Romance
92 minutes
PG


Robert Malone (Martin Landau, *Ed Wood*) is a lonely, depressed senior citizen who lives alone and works at the local grocery store. Robert's life takes a turn for the better when Mary (Ellen Burstyn, *The Last Picture Show*) moves into the house across the street from him and asks him out for a date.

Robert hasn't dated for years and is incredibly nervous. He seeks advice from a young coworker, Mike (Adam Scott, *Parks and Recreation*), on dating and love. The two come up with a plan for Robert's special evening. Mary's daughter (Elizabeth Banks, *Pitch Perfect*) disapproves of the whole idea and tries to discourage her mom from going on the date. She doesn't want her mother to get hurt.

Actress Ellen Burstyn and Actor Martin Landau in a scene from *Lovely, Still*.
Photo Credit: Overture Street Films / Laura Von Roenn

*Lovely, Still* is about family, respect, and love. Over the years I had the chance to discuss this movie with Academy Award winner Martin Landau. He stated that he knew he wanted to play the role of Robert during his first read-through of the script. He was shocked that it was written by a nineteen-year-old, first-time scriptwriter Nicholas Fackler. Landau immediately called Academy Award winner Ellen Burstyn to play the role of Mary.

Both Burstyn's and Landau's performances are compellingly believable and pull at your heartstrings. Landau told me Robert Malone was one of the favorite roles of his lifetime. His powerful portrayal shines on the screen.

At the time of the filming, Ellen Burstyn ran the Actors Studio in New York, and Martin Landau ran the Actors Studio in Los Angeles. Watching two masters of their craft in one movie is a cinematic learning lesson for any aspiring actor.

Mary has a wonderful line in the movie that we can all learn from: "The past is something we cannot do anything about."

*Lovely, Still* was Nicholas Fackler's directorial debut and what an opportunity to work with such an amazing ensemble cast. Fackler's work was nominated for Best First Screenplay at the 2011, Film Independent Spirit Awards.

Have a box of Kleenex close by when you watch this precious independent film.


**27. *Mary and Max* (2009)**
Director: Adam Elliot
Animation/Dark Comedy
92 minutes
Not Rated


*Mary and Max* is based on a true story. Dr. Bernard Hazelhof says, "True friendship is seen through the heart, not the eyes."

Most people think animated films are made for children, but *Mary and Max* is not for kids. Don't let the Claymation scare you away from this film. It is a dark comedy that will make you laugh, cringe, and cry.

Mary Daisy Dinkle (Bethany Whitmore, *Girl Asleep*) is a lonely eight-year-old girl who lives in Melbourne, Australia, with her alcoholic mother and reclusive father. She asks her dad where babies come from; he replies that men sometimes find them at the bottom of their beer glasses.

Mary does not believe this answer and begins a mission to find a better response. While Mary is at the post office with her mother, who is stealing envelopes, she finds a New York City phone book. As she reads the names of Americans, she decides to randomly choose one individual to write to.

That random person is Max Jerry Horowitz, a lonely, obese, forty-four-year-old Jewish man with Asperger's syndrome. She writes, "Where do babies come from?" Through their letters, Mary and Max discover that they both love chocolate and a TV show called *The Noblets*.

This unlikely pair become pen pals for the next twenty years. They enrich each other's lives over the years, in good times and bad.

Max, voiced by the late Oscar winner Philip Seymour Hoffman (*Capote*), deals with anxiety every time he receives a letter from Mary. With the help of his therapist, Dr. Bernard Hazelhof (Adam Elliot, *Harvie Krumpet*), Max overcomes his angst and writes back. Mary is always excited to receive a letter from Max. When she is older (and voiced by Toni Collette, *Little Miss Sunshine*), she makes a big mistake that Max views as a betrayal.

Will the two friends ever meet?

Hoffman is excellent in voicing Max, an extraordinarily complicated character. Hoffman's performance is award winning. What else would you expect from one of the greatest actors of all time?

Elliot's script is humorous, caring, and touching. This movie deals with difficult subjects in a caring manner. The letters discuss loneliness, mental illness, alcoholism, and bullying.

Elliot's choice of childlike Claymation characters and the use of colors in key moments in the film will aid you through the difficult situations that Max and Mary experience. He won an Oscar in 2004 for Best Short Film, Animated, for *Harvie Krumpet*.

**28. *The Mighty Macs* (2009)**
Director: Tim Chambers
Drama
99 minutes
G

I often wonder why some inspirational sports movie make it big, like *Rocky* or *Rudy*, while others remain obscure. *The Mighty Macs* is one of those sports film that didn't get much exposure when it came out in 2009.

In the early 1970s, a young basketball coach, Cathy Rush (Carla Gugino, *Spy Kids*), answers an ad for a head-coaching job at Immaculata College, a small all-girl Catholic college located in Pennsylvania. Cathy is offered the position by Mother Superior Saint John, portrayed by Oscar winner Ellen Burstyn (*Alice Doesn't Live Here Anymore*).

Soon after Cathy accepts the offer, at a salary of $450 for the season, she discovers that the school has no gymnasium; it was recently burned to ground. As if the missing gym were not enough, the school only has one basketball and is in financial trouble.

Mother Saint John's biggest concern is not about having a winning basketball team but controlling the girl's hormones.

Cathy's support at home is nonexistent. She is married to NBA referee Ed Rush (David Boreanaz, *Bones*). Her husband does not understand why she wants to be basketball coach. Supported or not, this job is something that Cathy really wants; she's dealing with the aftermath of a playing career cut short.

First, she must assemble a team, which is a challenge. With the help of an appointed assistant coach, Sister Sunday (Marley Shelton, *Grindhouse*), Cathy reaches her first goal. The bigger question is how Immaculata College will be able to compete against much larger schools in the division. When it seems, they don't have a prayer, Cathy tells the girls, "Anything can happen when we are committed to our dreams."

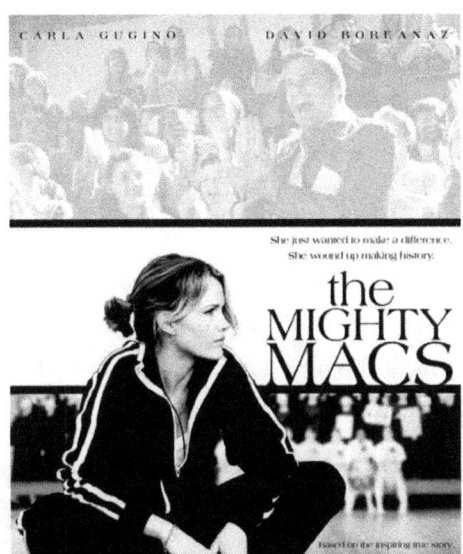

*The Mighty Macs* was the audience favorite at the 2010 California Independent Film Festival. Seven members of the 1972 Immaculata College team played nuns in the film. *The Mighty Macs* is rated G and can be enjoyed by the entire family. Get ready to cheer for the first-ever Cinderella story in women's basketball.

**29.** *Flipped* (2010)
Director: Rob Reiner
Comedy/Drama
90 minutes
PG

*Flipped*, based on the novel of the same name, is one of the most overlooked coming-of-age films in cinematic history. This charming film directed by Rob Reiner (*Stand By Me*) only grossed $2.4 million at movie theaters worldwide.

Prior to the start of the school, Bryce (Callan McAuliffe, *The Walking Dead*), a soon-to-be second grader, moves into a charming neighborhood. The first person to welcome Bryce is Juli (Madeline Carroll, *Mr. Popper's Penguins*), a girl of the same age who lives across the street. Bryce's stunning blue eyes make Juli quickly fall for him. As with any seven-year-old boy, Bryce is not interested in Juli or any girl, for that matter.

From the first scene, you learn how the film got its name, *Flipped*. Director Reiner shoots the scene in Juli's point of view, and then again in Bryce's interpretation. This method is used throughout the movie. It shows what we all know girls and boys think differently.

Director Rob Reiner at the Los Angeles premiere of *Flipped* at the Cinerama Dome, Hollywood. July 26, 2010
Photo Credit: Paul Smith / Featureflash.com

We jump six years ahead and find Juli and Bryce now entering the eighth grade. Their interests have flipped, but Juli and Bryce are still seeing things from completely opposite viewpoints. As much as Bryce tries to make Juli like him, he constantly comes up short. Although Bryce's grandfather, Chet (John Mahoney, *Frasier*) doesn't say too much, Bryce soon learns Chet has a lot of wisdom.

Reiner is a master at assembling a believable cast in his films, and *Flipped* does not disappoint. Bryce's parents (Rebecca De Mornay, *The Hand that Rocks the Cradle*, and Anthony Edwards, *ER*) and Juli's parents (Penelope Ann Miller, *The Artist*, and Aidan Quinn, *Benny & Joon*), as supporting characters, makes the overall casting work. The character development in the script results in the audience knowing and feeling for each one.

The music score by six-time Oscar nominee Marc Shaiman (*Sleepless in Seattle*, *The American President*, *Patch Adams*, *Mary Poppins Returns*) is outstanding and takes you back to a less complicated time.

If you are a fan of Rob Reiner, *Stand By Me,* or the television show *The Wonder Years*, *Flipped* could become one of your favorite films. It is one of mine.

**30. *Bernie*** (2011)
Director: Richard Linklater
Drama/Comedy
104 minutes
PG-13

"Truth is stranger than fiction," wrote Mark Twain. *Bernie*, based on the true story of a murder in the small Texas town of Carthage, helps prove this statement. The film cuts to documentary-style interviews with residents to get their opinions of the events that changed their rural town. These intercuts are effective and enjoyable.

I will not give away the plot; I want you to enjoy the many bizarre twists and turns of the story. Jack Black (*School of Rock*) plays Bernie Tiede, the local assistant in the Carthage funeral home and the most beloved resident in town. He is the person involved in everything in the community: singing in church each week, directing, and performing in the local theater, and comforting the locals with any needed support.

This is the best performance of Jack Black's career. It is stellar when an actor makes you forget all his other roles and pulls you into a new character. Black received a Golden Globe nomination for this role, which was considerably warranted.

Oscar recipient Shirley MacLaine (*Terms of Endearment*), as Marjorie Nugent, is the meanest, wealthiest, and most hated person in Carthage. A special friendship develops between Marjorie and Bernie. Where their friendship goes is as strange as these two individuals. Oscar winner Matthew McConaughey (*Dallas Buyers Club*) portrays the local DA, Danny Buck. The movie is written and directed by Texas native and five-time Oscar nominee Richard Linklater (*Before Sunset, Before Midnight, Boyhood*).

The film received two Film Independent Spirt Award in 2013 for Best Feature and Best Actor for Jack Black.

If you are looking for a unique film that will leave you saying, "Really?" then *Bernie* is the movie for you.

**31. *Carnage* (2011)**
Director: Roman Polanski
Comedy/Drama
80 minutes
R

You can probably remember a few scuffles you had when you were a kid. Your dad's response may have been, "Did you hit him good?" Your mom probably said, "Poor baby. Let me make it better and ease the pain in your black eye."

Society has changed with today's numerous lawsuits. This is what *Carnage* is all about: parents overreacting. It deals with the parents' reactions after their sons have a confrontation at the neighborhood park. Sometimes parents have a hard time letting go, while the kids just brush the incident off.

*Carnage* is based on the play *God of Carnage*, by Yasmina Reza. The film is directed by Oscar recipient Roman Polanski (*The Pianist*). It is a true art film, shot mainly in one location with a cast of four. For a movie as compartmentalized as *Carnage*, the cast has to be stellar and deliver outstanding performances to be successful.

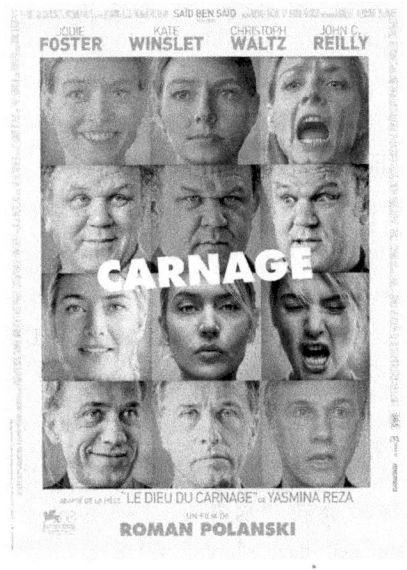

This cast features some of the big guns of Hollywood: two-time Oscar winner, Jodie Foster (*The Accused, The Silence of the Lambs*), Oscar winner, Kate Winslet (*The Reader*), two-time Oscar winner, Christoph Waltz (*Inglourious Basterds, Django Unchained*), and Oscar nominee, John C. Reilly (*Chicago*). Jodi Foster and Kate Winslet each received Golden Globe nominations for their exceptional performances.

There are several funny moments, and if you are a parent, you will without question relate to the overreaction to a situation involving your child.

*Carnage* is worth a watch. You will have a few laughs at the film, or at yourself as a parent.

**32. *Submarine*** (2010)
Director: Richard Ayoade
Comedy/Drama
97 minutes
R

Oliver Tate (Craig Roberts, *22 Jump Street*) is a quirky Welsh teenager with a vivid imagination. The opening scene has Oliver daydreaming in class as his teacher is discussing self-discovery. We hear Oliver's voice-over saying, "The only way to get through life is to picture myself in an entirely disconnected reality."

Oliver envisions the reactions of his classmates, parents, and society if he dies. This is the prologue of the movie. The film goes on for three acts and an epilogue.

The plot focuses on two goals Oliver has set for himself: losing his virginity before his sixteenth birthday and trying to keep his parents from getting a divorce. Oliver finds himself at the crossroad between childhood and adulthood. He is dealing with his first love, Jordana (Yasmin Paige, *I Could Never Be Your Woman*), a mischievous, feisty, straight-talking girl, and all the drama that comes along with this time in life. Oliver learns that Jordana is also dealing with trauma at home.

He is obsessed with protecting his parents' marriage. His father (Noah Taylor, *Shine*), is a depressed marine biologist. He assumes his mother, played by two-time Oscar nominee Sally Hawkins (*Blue Jasmine, The Shape of Water*), is no longer interested in sex, as the dimmer switch in their bedroom hasn't been set to the in-the-mood level for some time. Could his mother be having an affair with the neighbor Graham (Paddy Considine, *In America*), a charming spiritual guru?

The period of the film is not defined by Ayoade, which was a unique decision. The absence of cell phones in the school and the use of cassette players and VCRs suggest it is the late 1970s. Not identifying the period adds mystery to both Oliver and Jordana.

Craig Roberts, in his first lead role, gives a breakout performance as Oliver, a convoluted, multidimensional, and challenging character to portray. Yasmin Page's performance of Jordana is equally compelling. She is an individual who is seductive, compassionate, and enigmatic.

The cinematography by Erik Wilson (*Paddington*) is so terrific that it is an added character in the story line. The shots Wilson pulls out from a decaying town complements the feelings and emotions that all the characters are living through.

*Submarine* is a dark British comedy from first-time director Richard Ayoade. Film historians have described *Charade* as the best non-Hitchcock Hitchcock film. *Submarine* could be described as the best non-Wes Anderson Wes Anderson film. (Please don't repeat that to Richard Ayoade.) The script was adapted from the novel of the same title by Joe Dunthorne, published in 2008.

Richard Ayoade received an Outstanding Debut by a British Writer, Director, or Producer Award at the 2012 British Academy Film Awards. At the 2011 British Independent Film Awards (BIFA), *Submarine* was presented with the Douglas Hickox Award for Best Debut Director (Richard Ayoade). It also received four nominations for Best Screenplay (Ayoade), Best Supporting Actress (Sally Hawkins), and Most Promising Newcomer (Craig Roberts and Yasmin Page), and Richard Ayoade won the Best Screenplay.

*Submarine* is a coming-of-age film that reminds us that the paths we choose in our youth, often determines whom we become as adults.

**33. *Win Win* (2011)**
Director: Tom McCarthy
Drama/Comedy
106 minutes
R

*Win Win* stars two-time Golden Globe winner and Oscar nominee Paul Giamatti (*Cinderella Man, Sideways*) as Mike, a small-town attorney who is struggling to make ends meet. To try and improve his current financial situation, Mike decides to become the guardian of one of his clients, Leo (Burt Young, *Rocky*), who is in the early stages of dementia. When Leo is moved to a senior-living facility, Mike does not fully understand the ramifications.

The day Leo is transferred to the senior center, his runaway teenage grandson Kyle (Alex Shaffer, *Delinquent*) shows up at Leo's now-vacant home. Mike and his wife, Jackie, portrayed by Oscar nominee, Amy Ryan (*Gone Baby Gone*) agree to let Kyle stay at the home until they can contact his absentee mother.

Mike soon discovers that Kyle is a top-notch high school ranked wrestler from Ohio. Mike is the local volunteer high school wrestling coach, and it appears to be the perfect match. Mike's team has not won a wrestling tournament all season, but with Kyle in the lineup, that begins to change.

Things appears to be moving in the right direction until Leo's estranged daughter, Kyle's mother, comes to town.

*Win Win* was written and directed my Tom McCarthy, one of the greatest screenwriters of the 2000s. McCarthy won an Academy Award in 2016 for Best Writing, Original Screenplay for *Spotlight*, which he also directed. He has two films reviewed in this book, the most of any screenwriter: *The Station Agent* and *Win Win*. McCarthy is the king of independent film writing and directing.

McCarthy, as in all his films, has assembled a solid cast. Mike's best friend, Terry (Bobby Cannavale, *The Station Agent*) delivers great comedy. As in McCarthy's *The Station Agent*, Cannavale adds depth to *Win Win*. McCarthy's scripts also incorporate detailed character development, and this movie does not disappoint. He received a Best Screenplay nomination at the 2012 Film Independent Spirit Awards. His talent as a writer and director makes you care for each character, which makes *Win Win* a win.

**34.** *Frankenweenie* (2012)
Director: Tim Burton
Animation
87 minutes
PG

This story is about a boy and his dog, which touches the heart as it explores their relationship. There is a nod to the classic horror film *Frankenstein*. John August wrote the screenplay and has teamed up with Tim Burton several times for *Big Fish*, *Charlie and the Chocolate Factory*, *Corpse Bride*, and *Dark Shadows*.

This detailed, and beautifully produced stop-motion animation gives the entire film great depth. The 3-D element did not add anything to the movie, as the beauty of the artwork stands alone in 2-D.

In addition to Oscar recipient, Martin Landau (*Ed Wood*), the voice talent includes Catherine O'Hara (*Beetlejuice*, *Home Alone*), Martin Short (*Saturday Night Live*), two-time Oscar nominee, Winona Ryder (*Little Women*, *The Age of Innocence*), and Charlie Tahan (*Charlie St. Cloud*).

Tim Burton has delivered great films, including *Ed Wood*, *Beetlejuice*, and *Edward Scissorhands*. When *Frankenweenie* aired in 2012, I had the opportunity to interview Martin Landau. He said, "This is Tim's [Burton's] best work." I would have to agree. Mr. Landau lent his vocal talent as one of the lead characters, Mr. Rzykruski. As always, Landau was outstanding with his Vincent Price-type portrayal.

*Frankenweenie* is one of Tim Burton's greatest projects not only for its story but also for the visual masterpiece he created, with strong attention to detail in both the picture and the voices.

In 2013, *Frankenweenie* was nominated for an Oscar and a Golden Globe for Best Animated Feature.

*Frankenweenie* is a project that Tim Burton started as a short film when he was studying animation at California Institute of Art, forty years ago. Burton's stop-motion animation in black and white pays homage to such classics as *Frankenstein* and *Dracula*.

Do not miss *Frankenweenie*. Watching it with a child will give you an added treat.

Martin Landau at the premiere of his movie *Frankenweenie* at the El Capitan Theatre, Hollywood, CA. September 24, 2012
Photo Credit: Paul Smith / Featureflash.com

**35. *The Sapphires*** (2012)
Director: Wayne Blair
Comedy/Drama
103 minutes
PG-13

*The Sapphires* is a celebration of Motown music that will have you tapping your feet from the beginning to the end. Inspired by a true story, *The Sapphires* has its world premiere at the 2012 Cannes Film Festival.

*The Sapphires* takes place in 1968, where an R&B loving music manager from Ireland named Dave Lovelace, played by Irish comedian Chris O'Dowd (*Bridesmaids*), is looking for his next big musical act. Lovelace comes across three young aboriginal sisters singing at a talent show in Australia. As the sisters are performing, they are taunted with racial slurs by the audience.

They are clearly the best act but are not awarded the victory due to the color of their skin. After the show, the sisters plead with Lovelace to help them launch their careers. The girls move from county music to soul; they slip on the go-go boots Motown-style, and the new Sapphires are ready to take the stage.

Jessica Mauboy, Miranda Tapsell, Chris O'Dowd, Shari Sebbens and Deborah Mailman arriving for the London Film Festival screening of *The Sapphires*, at Odeon West End, London. October 15, 2012
Photo Credit: Featureflash.com

Lovelace can only find them a gig in Vietnam entertaining the US troops. Soon it's off to Vietnam, but first they stop in Melbourne to locate a fourth singer. Kay was a victim of the Australian government's cruel involuntary adoption policy of aboriginal children, which continued until the 1970s.

*The Sapphires* was Australian director Wayne Blair's debut. He does an admirable job with the formulaic script. The singing quartet is mainly comprised of newcomers who perform as veterans of the big screen. Chris O'Dowd shines in this film.

*The Sapphires* won eleven Australian Academy of Cinema and Television Art (AACTA) Awards in 2013, including Best Film.

If you are looking for fun, lighthearted movie with great music, *The Sapphires* will hit the right chord.

**36. *Fading Gigolo*** (2013)
Director: John Turturro
Comedy
90 minutes
R

If you are looking for a sophisticated comedy, I highly recommend the independent film *Fading Gigolo*, written and directed by and starring veteran actor John Turturro (*Quiz Show*, *The Big Lebowski*).

Turturro plays a Manhattan floral designer, Fioravante, who agrees to become a professional Don Juan to help his best friend, Murray, portrayed by Woody Allen (*Annie Hall*, *Hannah and Her Sisters*, *Midnight in Paris*), make a few extra dollars. That's right: Woody Allen is John Turturro's pimp. The friends quickly find themselves in a triangle of love and money. The film costars Sharon Stone (*The Mighty*) and Sofia Vergara (*Modern Family*).

When the film came out in 2013, I had the pleasure of interviewing John Turturro. He explained that he worked and reworked the script for over a year while openly taking input and corrective suggestions from the master of sophisticated comedy scripts, Woody Allen. When Allen agreed to play the role of Murray, Turturro knew he had something special.

I asked him what the biggest obstacle was in making an independent film, being the writer, director, and star on the project. He had a quick response:

"Time," he said. The movie was shot in a little over six weeks. "We had to prepare, prepare, and prepare." He credits his preparation with Woody, which helped in completing the film within the short shooting schedule.

One of my favorite scenes in film is when Murray teaches a few young boys how to play baseball. The dialogue between Woody and the boys is priceless. John said he came up with idea while watching dads trying to teach their sons baseball in the park across the street from his Brooklyn home.

*Fading Gigolo* has a fast ninety-minute running time and will make you laugh out loud. This comedy is an excellent example of what all independent filmmakers strive for.

**37. *Locke*** (2013)
Director: Stephen Knight
Drama
85 minutes
R

Here is a movie that is completely different.

*Locke* is perfect for those aspiring filmmakers who often ask me, "What is the key to producing a low-budget film?" My response is always, "Limited cast, no kids, no animals, no stunts, no special effects, no CGI (computer-generated images), limited locations, and a compelling, unique script." Most would say without those elements there would not be a movie.

*Locke* has all the above and even takes it to more of an extreme level with only one actor, Tom Hardy (*The Revenant*), and one location, the interior of his car. Sound intriguing? It should. The film begins with Ivan Locke (Hardy) leaving the construction site where he is a supervisor. It is the eve of a massive concrete pour, with over two hundred trucks scheduled for the next day. As soon as he gets into his BMW, he begins a series of telephone calls that will change his life forever.

The string of calls Ivan makes and receives are emotional, intense, realistic, and gripping. Each conversation builds the suspense of a guy who is about to lose everything: his family, his job, and his own self-worth. The entire movie never leaves the car and is basically in real time. The drive to his location is hour and fifteen minutes: almost the exact running time for the movie. There are some exterior shots, but most of the film is just Ivan driving down the freeway.

How can this movie not feel claustrophobic? It has a fresh, intense script, written by Stephen Knight, and an authentic acting performance by Tom Hardy—that's how. It is difficult to pull off a one-person play, but a movie is nearly impossible. I can't even think of another movie with a cast of *one*. Plus, the cinematography, with the use of rain shots and colorful reflections of car and building lights, adds to the tension and suspense of the movie. Hardy's performance was pretty much overlooked in 2003. The only accolade he received was a Best Actor Award from the Los Angeles Film Critics.

*Locke* receive no attention in the United States but did receive a Best Independent British Film Award. *Locke* is a movie that addresses how one wrong decision can alter a life.

Tom Hardy arrives for the premiere of *Locke* which is being screened at the Odeon West End as part of the BFI London Film Festival 2013.
Photo Credit: Featureflash.com

**38. *Parkland* (2013)**
Director: Peter Landesman
Drama/History
93 minutes
PG-13

Parkland is the hospital in Dallas, Texas, where President John F. Kennedy was taken after his assassination. Although millions have seen footage of the shooting, few are familiar with the many individuals whose lives were so tragically changed on November 22, 1963.

*Parkland* portrays the people (hospital personnel, first responders, FBI, reporters, et cetera) who were affected by the assassination. A young resident, Dr. Charles "Jim" Carrico (Zac Efron) finds himself trying to save the life of the president of the United States, and less than thirty-six hours later, finds himself in the same situation with Lee Harvey Oswald, the assassin. It was Nurse Doris Nelson, played by Oscar winner Marcia Gay Harden (*Pollock, The Mist*), who had to deal with the hospital staff, CIA agents, and FBI agents as she was trying to keep it all together.

There was the Zapruder video, but who was Abraham Zapruder (Paul Giamatti, *Cinderella Man)?* Giamatti always delivers an amazing performance. In this movie he makes you feel for Zapruder, who carries the burden of shooting a home video that haunts him for the rest of his life.

First-time director Peter Landsman, a former journalist, does an excellent job of making the audience believe they are with Zapruder and filming the motorcade, in the total chaos of the emergency room, and at the swearing-in on Air Force One. The use of original footage creates elements of realism and tension as you are drawn into the chaotic environment.

Other cast members include Oscar winner Billy Bob Thornton (*Sling Blade*) as secret service agent Forrest Sorrels and Oscar nominee Jacki Weaver (*Silver Linings Playbook*) as Marguerite Oswald, mother of Lee Harvey Oswald. While watching the film, I thought she was overacting. After researching footage of Marguerite Oswald on YouTube, I realized Weaver nailed it! Her performance of Marguerite was dead on. Equally as good was James Badge Dale (*World War Z*) as Robert Oswald, Lee Harvey's brother.

*Parkland* is a movie that makes one realize how one event can change so many lives forever.


**39. *The Spectacular Now* (2013)**
Director: James Ponsoldt
Drama/Comedy
95 minutes
R


Miles Teller (*Whiplash*) plays Sutter, a high school senior who appears to have it all. He's dating Cassidy, the most beautiful girl in school, portrayed by Oscar winner Brie Larson (*Room*). The party does not start until he shows up. Everyone seems to love him and want to be with him.

As graduation approaches, things start to unravel for Sutter. He begins to question himself. After a night of binge drinking, Sutter is found asleep on a stranger's lawn. Aimee (Shailene Woodley, *The Descendants*), who lives at home with her overly protective mother, wakes him up. She recognizes Sutter from school, but he has no idea who she is.

Aimee is "the nice girl" at school and is not in with the popular kids. She is simple. Sutter begins to know Aimee and finds that he really likes her. No one at school can figure out why Sutter would be with Aimee. Even Sutter's best friend, Ricky (Masam Holden, *Me and Earl and the Dying Girl*), questions him and says, "You are just going to hurt her."

Aimee dreams of the future, while Sutter lives for now. She directly and indirectly assists Sutter in finding himself. Along the way Sutter discovers hardships, disappointments, and struggles.

Miles Teller is one of the best actors of the 2000s and in my opinion is overlooked and underappreciated. His performance in *The Spectacular Now* is rare, real, and relatable. He won the Dramatic Special Jury Award for Acting at the 2013 Sundance Film Festival for his role as Sutter.

Shailene Woodley's portrayal of Aimee is also top notch. She plays the quiet, naive, and innocent young girl perfectly. Throughout the movie she pulls you in. You find yourself rooting for her and hoping she will not be disappointed by Sutter.

*The Spectacular Now* is a movie that everyone should see especially high schoolers. It's a coming-of-age film that deals with the inner struggles of adolescence. A person may appear to be the life of the party but may be hurting inside. As the old saying goes, "Never judge a book by its cover." There is a twist in the middle of the movie that is one of most unexpected turns in film history one that will leave you gasping.

*The Spectacular Now* was a Sundance Film Festival favorite in 2013, where it was nominated for the Grand Jury Prize. The film also received two Film Independent Spirit Award nominations in 2014: Best Female Lead (Shailene Woodley) and Best Screenplay (Scott Neustadter and Michael H. Weber).

Although the movie only grossed $6.9 million at the box office, *The Spectacular Now* remains one of many favorites and should be seen.

**40. *Chef*** (2014)
Director: Jon Favreau
Comedy/Drama
114 minutes
R

Carl Casper (Jon Favreau, *Iron Man*) is one of the top chefs in Los Angles. The restaurant's owner, Riva (Dustin Hoffman, *Rain Man*), is suppressing Carl's creative talents. Their conflict comes to a head when restaurant critic and blogger Ramsey Michel (Oliver Platt, *West Wing*) plans his next review. Things don't go as planned, and on a return visit by Ramsey, Carl is out of a job.

Carl's ex-wife Inez, played by four-time Golden Globe nominee Sofia Vergara (*Modern Family*), has always encouraged him to own a food truck. There he can showcase his creative aptitude for cooking and have total control in his kitchen. Out of desperation, Carl reluctantly agrees and receives a beat-up old taco truck from Inez's ex, Marvin (Robert Downey Jr., *Chaplin*), who lives in Miami.

It's the restoration of the food truck and the bonding with Carl's young son, Percy (Emjay Anthony, *It's Complicated*), that adds sweetness to the film. On their journey from Miami to Los Angeles, father and son teach each other that the most important gift anyone can give is their time. They are joined on the journey with friend and coworker Martin, portrayed by Golden Globe nominee, John Leguizamo (*To Wong Foo Thanks for Everything, Julie Newmar*).

If you have an appetite for a superior food movie, then see *Chef*. Just don't watch it on an empty stomach. The numerous culinary scenes will result in your stomach growling during the entire time. *Chef* is written by, directed by, and stars Jon Favreau. He knows how to prepare a film that Hollywood's elite would jump through hoops to be in. His track record as a director is the result of using star-studded casts in the films *Swingers*, *Elf*, and the first two *Iron Man* movies.

*Chef* is filled with A-listers, including two-time Oscar nominee Scarlett Johansson (*Jojo Rabbit*, *Marriage Story*), Robert Downey Jr., John Leguizamo, Sofia Vergara, and two-time Oscar winner Dustin Hoffman (*Kramer vs. Kramer*, *Rain Man*).

*Chef* has all the right ingredients: comedy, solid performances by elite actors, and a sweet, well-written script. It's worth a second helping.

**41. *Mr. Turner* (2014)**
Director: Mike Leigh
Biography, Drama
150 minutes
R

*Mr. Turner* is a true story that examines the later years in the life of the brilliant and peculiar nineteenth-century British painter J. M. W. Turner. The film centers around the philosophical change the death of his father had on Turner and his personal relationships.

Veteran British actor Timothy Spall's (*Secrets & Lies*) performance of the complex and curmudgeonly Turner is exceptional. This portrayal is an excellent character study for any aspiring actor. In most years Spall would have been nominated for an Oscar, but the 2015 Best Actor category was probably the strongest in Oscar history. I am sure Mr. Turner is groaning over the missed nomination.

The film was written and directed by seven-time Oscar nominee Mike Leigh (*Secrets & Lies*, *Vera Drake*). Leigh accurately delivers the film through the eyes of Turner. The audience sees what this brilliant artist saw, from just the right sunset to the perfect landscape.

The London Film Critics Circle awarded *Mr. Turner* seven nominations, the highest for any film in 2015. *Mr. Turner* was nominated for four Academy Awards: Best Cinematography (Dick Pope), Best Costume Design (Jacqueline Durran), Best Production Design (Suzie Davies, Charlotte Dirickx), and Best Original Score (Gary Yershon). These nominations alone should tell you that *Mr. Turner* is worth the time to watch.

Do not miss this gorgeous piece of art. Every landscape, sunset, seascape, and valley in film appears as if the actors are standing in a masterpiece. This is cinematography at its best, a visual treat. I believe film schools should use *Mr. Turner* as a case study for brilliance in cinematography.

I recommend *Mr. Turner* not just for great storytelling, but also for the stunning beauty of every shot in the film, which is a painting unto its own. This film is truly a piece of art, one that would please J. M. W. Turner.

Timothy Spall at the photocall for his new movie *Mr. Turner* at the 67th Festival de Cannes, May 15, 2014
Photo Credit: Paul Smith / Featureflash.com

**42. *St. Vincent*** (2014)
Director: Theodore Melfi
Comedy/Drama
102 minutes
PG-13

At first glance one might say that based on the cast (Bill Murray, Melisa McCarthy, and Naomi Watts), *St. Vincent* would be a slapstick comedy. It is far from that. It's a "dramedy" about a young boy named Oliver (Jaeden Lieberher, *It*), who is dealing with his parents' separation.

Oliver moves, enters a new school, and finds an unlikely friend in his new neighbor. Vincent is a grumpy, unhappy old man. It teaches a lesson all of us can learn from that there is good in all people.

*St. Vincent* is Jaeden's first role as an actor, and he does an excellent job opposite the veteran actors: Murray (*Lost in Translation*), McCarthy (*Bridesmaids*), and Watts (*The Impossible, 21 Grams*).

When *St. Vincent* was shown in 2014, I wrote in my movie review column, "Based on Jaeden's performance, we will see him for years to come." I was correct. Jaeden went on to change his name in the 2019 starring in *Knives Out* and television series, *Defending Jacob*. He is now credited under the name Jaeden Martell.

Murray's performance as Vincent was exceptional, and he received a Golden Globe nomination in 2015 for the role. In my opinion, he should have won the Golden Globe that year and received an Oscar nod.

First-time feature film director Theodore Melfi, who also wrote the screenplay, succeeded in his pitch, and Murray agreed to the role. He worked with Melfi on the script, and it truly shines on the big screen. Other supporting cast include Oscar nominee Terrance Howard (*Hustle & Flow*) and Chris O'Dowd (*Bridesmaids* and the 2012 gem *The Sapphires*).

*St. Vincent* was my favorite film of 2014. Do yourself a favor: see this wonderfully acted, scripted, and directed movie. If you are not touched by this movie, you have missed the point. This film will make you laugh, cry, and learn a valuable life lesson.


**43. *Me and Earl and the Dying Girl* (2015)**
Director: Alfonso Gomez-Rejon
Drama/Comedy
105 minutes
PG-13


I have often said that the script is the key to a quality movie. *Me and Earl and the Dying Girl* is a prime example of a script that is funny and endearing and pulls at your heartstrings. It was adapted from the 2012 best-selling novel of the same name by Jesse Andrews.

Greg (Thomas Mann, *Beautiful Creatures*) is an awkward eighteen-year-old dealing with growing pains, acceptance, and the everyday issues of a high school senior. When his parents (Connie Britton, *Nashville* and Nick Offerman, *Parks and Recreation*) learn that a girl in his class, Rachel (Olivia Cooke, *Ready Player One*) is dying of leukemia, they insist he visit her.

Greg is reluctant but soon finds himself at her front door. After an embarrassing first encounter at the staircase, Greg enters Rachel's bedroom. Socially inept, Greg often says things that are inappropriate or uncomfortable. His comments make Rachel laugh. Although he was reluctant to visit her at first, it becomes a daily ritual, and a friendship is built.

Greg's only friend at school is Earl (RJ Cyler, *Power Rangers*), who is a bit reclusive. The boys don't eat in the cafeteria but in the office of one of their teachers. Earl and Greg have been acquaintances for years, and their common bond is their love of filmmaking.

The boys make short film spoofs of classic movies such as *A Clockwork Orange* and *Midnight Cowboy*. After a while Greg introduces Earl to Rachel, and the three develop a unique friendship.

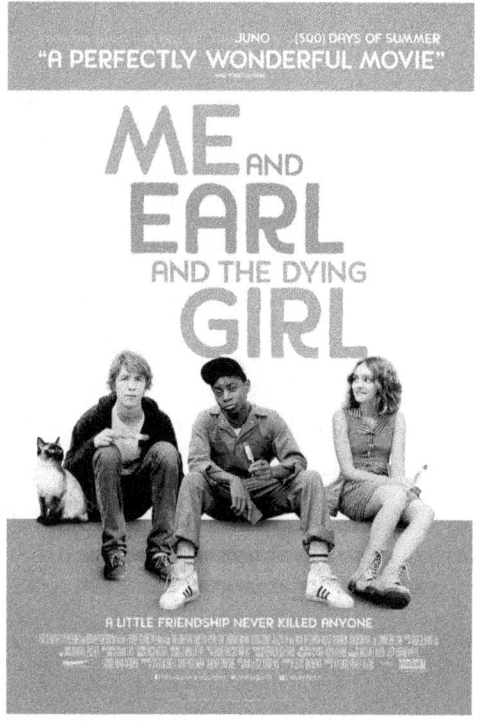

The ensemble cast is outstanding, which is vital for such a heavily dialogue-driven film. You will feel the multiple arcs of each characters, direct results of their performances.

*Me and Earl and the Dying Girl* won the Grand Jury Award and the Audience Award at the 2015 Sundance Film Festival and received a Film Independent Spirit Award nomination for Best First Screenplay for Jesse Andrews.

*Me and Earl and the Dying Girl* is indeed something special.

**44.** *Tab Hunter Confidential* (2015)
Director: Jeffrey Schwarz
Documentary
90 minutes
Not Rated

In the 1950s there were three leading men in Hollywood: James Dean, Rock Hudson, and Tab Hunter. Tab became Hollywood's golden boy.

Tab was discovered at the age of nineteen, and the Hollywood machine made him a star. He landed his first leading role opposite Linda Darnell in 1952 in the romantic South Sea adventure *Island of Desire*. From that time forward, the Hollywood marketing machine took over his life. They'd found their golden boy and capitalized on him.

Hunter starred in over forty studio films, including *Ride the Wild Surf* and the Academy Award-nominated film *Damn Yankees*. He also costarred opposite several screen legends including Sophia Loren, Natalie Wood, Rita Hayworth, Lana Turner, and Debbie Reynolds.

His film success was not enough for Hollywood, it was time to make more money off their newfound teen idol. Hunter had an amazing recording career with his song "Young Love," which soared to top of the record charts and knocked Elvis out of the top spot. *Young Love* remained the number-one record in the United States for six weeks, and Hunter became every teenage girl's dream. His popularity led him to his own television show on NBC, *The Tab Hunter Show*.

Hollywood created Hunter, but who was the real Tab Hunter? Tab had a secret that would destroy his career: he was gay.

This truthful documentary explores Tab's rise to stardom, his insecurities in the role, and the person Hollywood created. Based on the *New York Times* best-selling book of the same name, this amazing film tells the story of not only who the real Tab Hunter is, in his own words, but also exposes the roller-coaster life Hollywood created around him.

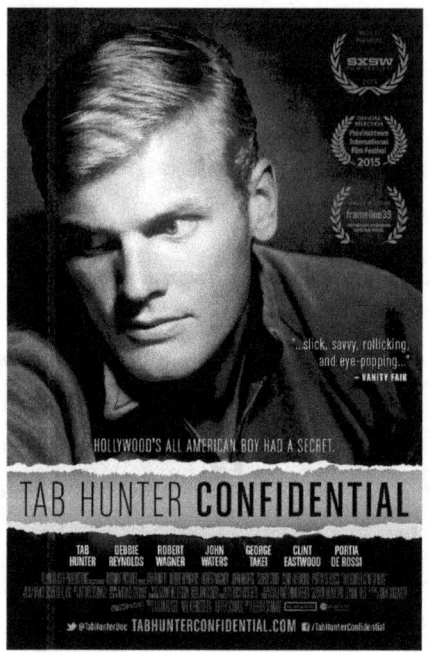

The use of vintage footage and modern technology makes this documentary special. Interviews with several of Tab's costars, including Debbie Reynolds, Clint Eastwood, George Takei, Connie Stevens, and director John Waters, are included.

*Tab Hunter Confidential* won Best Documentary at the 2015 California Independent Film Festival, and Tab was honored with a much-deserved Lifetime Achievement Award.


**45.** *Trumbo* (2015)
Director: Jay Roach
Biography/Drama
124 minutes
R

Dalton Trumbo (Bryan Cranston, *Breaking Bad*) was Hollywood's top screenwriter in 1947. He had already written thirty screenplays, produced from 1936 to 1945.

This number does not include the numerous scripts he worked on as a script polisher.

His career came to a screeching halt in 1947 when Trumbo and nine other Hollywood executives (*The Hollywood Ten*), were jailed and blacklisted after refusing to answer House Un-American Activities Committee questions about their alleged involvement with the Communist Party.

The ten men were each sentenced to one year in federal prison. Trumbo served ten months and was kicked out of the Screen Writers Guild. This action did not stop him. He began writing for a B-movie studio, King Brothers Productions, and won two Academy Awards, using Robert Rich as a pseudonym (*The Brave One*) and Ian McLellan Hunter as a front writer (*Roman Holiday*). How disappointing to win two Oscars for screenwriting and not be personally honored. In 2011, the Writers' Guild of America restored full screenplay credit to Trumbo for *Roman Holiday*.

Bryan Cranston at the US premiere of *Trumbo* at the Academy of Motion Picture Arts & Sciences, Beverly Hills. October 27, 2015
Photo Credit: Paul Smith / Featureflash.com

*Trumbo* is directed by Jay Roach (*Austin Powers*, *Meet the Fockers*, *Borat*). He takes John McNamara's screenplay to an entertaining level, addressing the who's who in Hollywood, including Edward G. Robinson (Michael Stuhlbarg, *A Serious Man*), John Wayne (David James Elliott, *JAG*), Kirk Douglas (Dean O'Gorman, *The Hobbit: An Unexpected Journey*), Otto Preminger (Christian Berkel, *Valkyrie*), and gossip columnist Hedda Hopper portrayed by Oscar recipient Helen Mirren (*The Queen*).

Bryan Cranston received both Oscar and Golden Globe nominations in 2016 for this role. Helen Mirren received a Golden Globe nomination for Best Performance by an Actress in a Supporting Role in a Motion Picture. John Goodman was overlooked during award season. His performance in the role of Frank King, a prolific B-movie producer known to swing a baseball bat in meetings, was an absolute standout in my opinion.

*Trumbo* not only addresses a dark period in Hollywood history but also explores Trumbo's family life. The film depicts the importance of having a supportive family in both good and bad times. *Trumbo* is a movie that conveys essential life lessons.


**46. *Sing Street*** (2016)
Director: John Carney
Comedy/Drama
106 minutes
PG-13


Conor (Ferdia Walsh-Peelo, *Vikings*), a fourteen-year-old boy who lives in Dublin, Ireland, is the main character in *Sing Street*. One day his parents inform him that due to the recession, he will have to leave private school and transfer to a less impressive inner-city public high school.

On his first day, he is bullied by classmates and scolded by the principal for not wearing black shoes. When he returns the next day still wearing brown shoes, he is told to remove his shoes and pick them up at the end of the day.

After school, he notices a stunning girl standing across the street. Conor strikes up a conversation and discovers that Raphina (Lucy Boynton, *Bohemian Rhapsody*) is an aspiring model who has plans to move to London. Conor asks if she would like to be in his band's upcoming music video. She agrees.

Conor now has a big problem: he does not have a band. He is on mission to win Raphina's heart, so he gathers the most unlikely group of boys to form a band. Conor names the band Sing Street, after the high school. He changes his name to Cosmo.

Conor is encouraged by his older brother, Brendan (Jack Reynor, *Midsommar*), a college dropout and hash smoker who always dreamed of becoming a musician. Watching the bond between the two siblings grow is touching.

*Sing Street* was written and directed by John Carney, who also directed *Once*, also reviewed in this book. Both films were inspired by Carney's love for music.

He has the ability to cast individuals who are natural and believable. He makes the viewer care for each character.

*Sing Street* was nominated for Best Motion Picture, Musical or Comedy, at the 2017 Golden Globes.

The soundtrack is what you would anticipate from a movie based in the 1980s with songs by Duran Duran, the Clash, Hall & Oates, and Genesis. *Sing Street* shows how music can transport you from everyday worries. If you are a fan of the 80s music scene, *Sing Street* hits the right notes.

**47. *Finding Your Feet* (2017)**
Director: Richard Loncraine
Comedy
111 minutes
PG-13

*Finding Your Feet* is an upbeat British comedy that will have you tapping your feet while you are viewing this fun film. The ensembled cast of veteran British actors is superb.

Lady Sandra Abbott, portrayed by Imelda Staunton (*Vera Drake*), makes a discovery at a retirement party for her husband of forty years. Mike Abbott (John Sessions, *The Good Shepherd*) has been having an affair with her best friend, Pamela (Josie Lawrence, *Enchanted April*) for years. Distraught, Lady Sandra has nowhere to turn except to her older sister Bif (Celia Imrie, *The Best Exotic Marigold Hotel*). They haven't been in contact in over a decade and are complete opposites. Lady Sandra is an upper-class snob, and Bif is a carefree, pot-smoking hippie. Lady Sandra has no other choice and is forced to move into her sister's tiny flat.

Bif tries to get her sister out of her funk and find her footing. She reminds her how much she enjoys dancing. Bif joins an eclectic group of seniors who become her extended family. The diverse students include an antique dealer

Charlie (Timothy Spall, *Mr. Turner*), his old buddy Ted (David Hayman, *Taboo*) and Jackie (Joanna Lumley, *Absolutely Fabulous*) as a recently divorced hottie.

Sandra realizes that she gave up her passion for dance to be a trophy wife for an affluent jerk. The dance group sautés the zest for life back into Sandra.

*Finding Your Feet* touches upon issues including marital problems, dying, dementia, loneliness, and the need for a sense of belonging. All of these topics are addressed in a humorous, lighthearted way. The music will lure you into this film with some of the greatest dance tunes of all time, such as "Rock around the Clock," "Chantilly Lace," "In the Mood," "Rockin' Robin," and "Le Freak."

*Finding Your Feet* will have you dancing and singing away.

**48. *Beautiful Boy*** (2018)
Director: Felix van Groeningen
Biography/Drama
120 minutes
R

*Beautiful Boy* is a true story based a pair of memoirs of a father and son. David and Nicolas (Nic) Sheff recount Nic's drug addiction and how it affects the entire family. It is a compelling and raw portrayal of drug addiction. This is a movie that you must prepare yourself to watch, much like *The Woodsman*.

Nic (Timothée Chalamet, *Call Me by Your Name*) is a high school student who appears to have it all. He is popular, a good student athlete, and editor of the school newspaper, and he aspires to becoming an actor.

When Nic becomes addicted to meth, everything seems to crumble around him and his dad. David (Steve Carell, *The Office*), a successful San Francisco journalist, will do everything in his power to save this son and his family. The movie weaves both books together, dramatizing the hell that both Nic and David went through in their battle with crystal meth.

Throughout the movie David refuses to stand back and watch his son spiral out of control. This is a no-win situation that pushes the limits of their relationship. Each time Nic seems to get back on track, he relapses. There is a scene in which David is searching for Nic, who is now living on the streets of San Francisco, that is heart-wrenching. David questions where he went wrong as a father. Knowing that his son could die at any time is destroying David.

Carell delivers a solid performance as a father struggling through the horrors of his son's drug addiction. Chalamet's performance and transformation are pure acting at its finest. The roller-coaster ride that he takes the audience on will bring out every human emotion in the viewer.

You will discover that Chalamet is the best actor of his generation. He received a Best Supporting Actor Golden Globe nomination but was overlooked at the Academy Awards. In my opinion, Chalamet should have won the Golden Globe and the Oscar in 2019.

*Beautiful Boy* is a film that was disappointingly overlooked due to the harsh subject matter. I believe it is worth seeing—if only to witness Chalamet's remarkable performance.

Have a box of tissues nearby.

Timothée Chalamet at the London Film Festival screening of *Beautiful Boy* at the Cineworld Leicester Square, London. October 13, 2018
Photo Credit: Featureflash.com

**49. *The Bill Murray Stories: Life Lessons Learned from a Mythical Man*** (2018)
Director: Tommy Avallone
Documentary
70 minutes
TV-MA

Everyone knows about the legendary Bigfoot sightings around the world, but have you heard about the Bigfootesque sightings of actor/comedian Bill Murray? The legend states that Murray will randomly appear in the most obscure locations and spend time with complete strangers.

Murray may be one of Hollywood's most untouchable actors when it comes to film roles. He doesn't even have an agent. If you want to offer Murray a role in your film, you must call his personal cell phone. Simply leave him a message, pitch the role, and hope for a call back.

Actor Bill Murray at the 58th Annual Film Festival de Cannes. May 17, 2005
Photo Credit: Paul Smith / Featureflash.com

But when it comes to nonbusiness, Bill may just show up in your kitchen, wash your dishes and help clean up, or photobomb your picture. This film documents a few of Murray's random acts of kindness.

You learn from the documentary that Murray has no interest in talking about his roles in films like *Caddyshack* or *Ghostbusters*. He loves spending time with people and discovering what makes them tick. He just wants to hang out and enjoy time spent with others.

*The Bill Murray Stories: Life Lessons Learned from a Mythical Man* is a fun-filled, laugh-out-loud documentary that explores how a simple act of kindness can make someone's day and create a memory they will talk about for years.

Watch this unique film, and you, too, will be sharing Murray sightings with family and friends. And who knows? Maybe Murray will be knocking at your front door soon.

**50.** *The Peanut Butter Falcon* (2019)
Directors: Tyler Nilson and Michael Schwartz
Comedy/Drama
97 minutes
PG-13

Zak portrayed by newcomer, Zack Gottsagen, is an adult male with Down Syndrome, has one dream in life: to become a professional wrestler. Zak has learned from the VHS wrestling tape that he views every day and night that his hero, Salt Water Redneck (Thomas Haden Church, *Sideways*), runs a professional wrestling training school in Florida. The only problem is that Zak lives in North Carolina.

After several failed attempts to run away from his care home, Zak asks his roommate, Carl (Bruce Dern, *Nebraska*), for help. Carl, who has watched the wrestling video one too many times, agrees to assist Zak. That evening Zak escapes the facility with the aid of Carl and heads off to Florida to fulfill his dream. Zak has no idea how to get to Florida.

Along his journey, Zak encounters Tyler (Shia LaBeouf, *Transformers*), who is also on the run. Tyler quickly takes a liking to Zak and agrees to take him to Florida. Their friendship grows stronger with every obstacle they overcome along the away.

The care home sends Eleanor (Dakota Johnson, *Fifty Shades of Grey*) to find Zak before the state, which holds custody of Zak, discovers that he has left the facility.

*The Peanut Butter Falcon* is a charming movie, with innocence that comes from Zack Gottsagen's natural and pure performance. This is his first acting major role and is a joy to see. One of the most genuine lines in the film, "Party" was ad-libbed by Zack.

The idea of the movie came about when the directors, Tyler and Michael, met Zack at a camp for disabled children. Zack told them his lifelong dream was to become a movie star. Tyler and Michael wrote the script around Zack, and his dream came true.

*The Peanut Butter Falcon* won the Audience Award for Narrative Spotlight at SXSW Film Fest 2019.

Zack Gottsagen at the 2020 Palm Springs International Film Festival Film Awards Gala.
Photo Credit: Paul Smith / Featureflash.com

*May movie theater marquees soon shine brightly again.*
Photo credit: Studio Dizon

Readers may contact Derek Zemrak via email or social media:

derek@zemrak.com
www.facebook.com/dzemrak
twitter.com/zemrak
Instagram@dzemrak

# Index

Numbers in **bold** indicate photographs

Affleck, Ben 38, **38**
Allen, Richard "Pistol" 23
Allen, Woody 61-62, **62**
Anderson, Gillian 12
Anderson, Wes 36, 37, 56
Andrews, Jesse 73, 74
Anthony, Emjay 68
Ashford, Jack 23
Astin, Sean 43
Avallone, Tommy 84
Ayoade, Richard 54, 55, 56

B-52's 1
Babbitt, Bob 23
Bacon, Kevin 34, **34**, 35
Bakula, Scott 9
Banks, Elizabeth 44
Bannen, Ian 14
Baumbach, Noah 35-36, 37
Baumgarten, Craig 28
*Beautiful Boy* 82-83
*Before Sunrise* 6-7
Benjamin, Benny "Papa Zita" 23
Benjamin, Paul 28
Berkel, Christian 78
*Bernie* 51-52, **52**
Besman, Michael 14

*Bill Murray Stories: The Life Lessons Learned from a Mythical Man* 84-85
Birch, Thora 18
Black, Jack 51, 52, **52**
Blair, Wayne 59, 61
Boothe, Powers 43
Boreanaz, David 48
Boyce, Frank Cottrell 32
Boyle, Danny 32
Boynton, Lucy 79
Bratt, Benjamin 34
Braugher, Andre 23
Britton, Connie 73
Broderick, Matthew 16
Brody, Adrien 37
Brown, Eddie "Bongo" 23
Burstyn, Ellen 7, 8, **8**, 44, 45, **45**, 48
Burton, Tim 58
Buscemi, Steve 18

Campbell, John J. 1
Cannavale, Bobby 29, 57
Carell, Steve 82
*Carnage* 53-54, **53**
Carney, John 41, 78, 79-80
Carrey, Jim 21, 22
Carroll, Madeline 50
Cates, Darlene 5
*Cats Don't Dance* 9-10, **10**
Chalamet, Timothée 82, 83, **83**
Chambers, Tim 48
*Chef* 68-69, **69**
Chelsom, Peter 11
Christensen, Hayden 26, **27**
Christensen, Tove 28
Church, Thomas Haden 85
Clarkson, Patricia 29
Clowes, Daniel 18
Collette, Toni 47
Considine, Paddy 55
Cooke, Olivia 73
Corwin, Charlie 37
Coulter, Allen 37
Craig, Dean 39
Cranston, Bryan 76, **77**, 78
Culkin, Kieran 11
Culkin, Rory 16, 30
Cyler, RJ 73

Parker, Laurie 2
*Parkland* 64-66, **65**
*Peanut Butter Falcon, The* 85-86
Peck, Josh 30-31
Peldon, Ashley 9
Phoenix, River 1, **2**
Pilkes, Hannah 35
Platt, Oliver 68
Polanski, Roman 53
Ponsoldt, James 66
Pope, Dick 70
"Private Idaho" 1
Quinn, Aidan 51

Ray, Billy 26, 28
Reeves, George 37-38
Reeves, Keanu 1, **2**
Reilly, John C. 54
Reiner, Rob 49, 50, **50**, 51
Reynolds, Debbie 75, 76
Reynor, Jack 79
Reza, Yasmina 53
Ricci, Christina 12, **13**, 14, 25
Roach, Jay 76, 78
Roberts, Craig 54, 55, 56
Roos, Don 12, 13, 14
Rowlands, Gena 11
Ruffalo, Mark 16
Ryan, Amy 56
Rydell, Mark 4
Ryder, Winona 58

*Sapphires, The* 59-61, 73
Sarsgaard, Peter 27, 28
Schroeder, Carly 30
Schwartz, Michael 85
Schwarz, Jeffrey 75
Scott, Adam 44
Sebbens, Shari **60**
Sedgwick, Kyra 34, 35
Sergei, Ivan 12
Sessions, John 80
Shaffer, Alex 56
Shaiman, Marc 51
*Shattered Glass* 26-28, **27**
Shelton, Marley 48
Short, Martin 58

*Sing Street* 78-80, **79**
Skalski, Mary Jane 30
Smith, Lois 37
Spacek, Sissy 19, **20**, 21
Spall, Timothy 70, **71**, 81
*Spectacular Now, The* 66-68, **67**
*Spitfire Grill, The* 7-8
*Squid and the Whale, The* 35-37, **36**
*St. Vincent* 71-73, **72**
Stafford, Bill 1
Stahl, Nick 19
*Standing in the Shadows of Motown* 23-24, **24**
Stanton, Harry Dean 11
*Station Agent, The* 28-30, **29**, 39, 57
Staunton, Imelda 80
Stevens, Connie 76
Sting 12
Stone, Sharon 11, **11**, 12, 61
Stuhlbarg, Michael 78
*Submarine* 54-56, **55**

*Tab Hunter Confidential* 75, **76**
Tahan, Charlie 58
Takei, George 76
Tapsell, Miranda **60**
Taylor, Noah 54
Teller, Miles 66, 67
Theron, Charlize 25, **26**
Thornton, Billy Bob 66
Tomei, Marisa 19, 21
*Trumbo* 76-78, **77**
Tunney, Robin 37
Turner, Lana 75
Turturro, John 61

Van Dyke, Earl 23
Van Sant, Gus 1
Vergara, Sofia 61, 68, 69

*Waking Ned Devine* 14-15, **15**
Walker, Mandy 28
Walsh-Peelo, Ferdia 78
Waltz, Christoph 54
Warfield, Emily 3
Waters, John 76
Watts, Naomi 71, 72
Weaver, Jacki 66

Weber, Michael H. 68
*What's Eating Gilbert Grape* 4-5
White, Robert 23
Whitmore, Bethany 46
Whitmore, James 22
Wilkinson, Tom 19, 21
Williams, Michelle 29
Willis, Eddie 23
Wilson, Erik 55
*Win Win* 29, 56-57, **57**
Winslet, Kate 54
Witherspoon, Reese **3**, 3, 4
Wood, Natalie 75
Woodley, Shailene 66, 67, 68
Woodman, Dave 10
*Woodsman, The* 34-35, **34**, 82

Yershon, Gary 70
*You Can Count on Me* 16-17, 35
Young, Burt 56

Zahn, Steve 28
Zlotoff, Lee David 7
Zwigoff, Terry 18